Better Homes Cookery

CALORIE COUNTER'S COOKBOOK

Sonia Allison

COLLINS LONDON AND GLASGOW

Contents

All spoon measures throughout the book, unless otherwise indicated, are level. For convenience, the approximation of 25 gm to the ounce has been used throughout this book.

Low-calorie Appetisers and Snacks

Mushroom Cocktail

38 calories per serving

4 tablespoons tomato ketchup
1 tablespoon vinegar
¼ level teaspoon prepared horseradish
Lettuce leaves and shredded lettuce
12 fresh medium mushrooms, sliced

In a small bowl blend ketchup, vinegar and horse-radish. Chill in the refrigerator. Line six glasses with lettuce leaves and half-fill with shredded lettuce. Add equal amounts of mushrooms to each. Before serving, coat with ketchup mixture. Serves 6.

Frosty Fruit Cup

66 calories per serving

1 can (1 lb or ½ kilo) pineapple chunks
¾ pint (375 ml) low-calorie bitter lemon
2 tablespoons fresh lime or lemon juice
Few drops of green food colouring
1 teacup seedless grapes
Melon balls from half a large melon
Mint sprigs (optional)

Drain pineapple, reserving syrup. Combine reserved syrup, bitter lemon, lime or lemon juice and colouring. Transfer to a 2½ pint refrigerator tray or two smaller ones. Freeze for 2 to 2½ hours or until mushy. Combine grapes and melon balls. Break frozen mixture up with a fork and spoon into eight sundae glasses. Top with pineapple, grapes and melon balls and, if liked, decorate with sprigs of mint. Serves 8.

Mushroom Cocktail, served in your most attractive glassware, makes a delicious and unusual first course.

Grapefruit and Crab Cocktail

57 calories per serving

The piquant sauce is delicious served over any shellfish

1 can (7½ oz or 187 gm) crab meat, chilled, drained, flaked, and cartilage removed
1 tablespoon lemon juice
1 can (1 lb or ½ kilo) grapefruit segments, chilled
4 tablespoons tomato ketchup
¼ level teaspoon dry mustard
¼ level teaspoon prepared horseradish
Dash of Tabasco sauce
Lettuce leaves

Sprinkle crab with lemon juice. Drain grapefruit, reserving 4 tablespoons syrup. Combine ketchup, reserved syrup, mustard, horseradish and Tabasco. Chill in the refrigerator. Arrange grapefruit and crab in lettuce-lined glasses, and coat with sauce. Serves 8.

Spiced Citrus Appetiser

52 calories per serving

A popular hors d'oeuvre but with a difference

1 can (1 lb or ½ kilo) mixed grapefruit and orange sections, undrained
3 inch stick cinnamon
Dash of ground cloves
Dash of ground ginger
Mint sprigs (optional)

In a saucepan combine grapefruit and orange sections, cinnamon stick, cloves and ginger; simmer for 10 minutes. Remove cinnamon stick and chill mixture in the refrigerator. Serve in glasses, garnished with mint sprigs, if liked. Serves 5.

8

Curried Chicken Soup

61 calories per serving

Serve either hot or cold

    1 can condensed cream of chicken soup
    ½ pint (250 ml) skimmed milk
    6 tablespoons water
    ½ teaspoon curry powder
    1 tablespoon chopped parsley

In a small saucepan gradually stir milk into soup. Add remaining ingredients. Heat till simmering, stirring occasionally. Garnish with additional chopped parsley, if liked. Serves 6.

Herbed Tomato Broth

22 calories per serving

    1 can condensed consommé
    ½ pint (250 ml) tomato juice
    ¼ pint (125 ml) water
    ¼ teaspoon dried marjoram
    ¼ teaspoon dried thyme
    1 tablespoon chopped parsley

Combine consommé, tomato juice, water, marjoram and thyme. Bring to boil. Reduce heat and simmer for 2 minutes. Ladle into bowls and garnish with parsley. Serves 6.

Tomato and Crab Bites

16 calories per appetizer

Serve on a bed of crushed ice

    3 tablespoons low-calorie dressing (see
      above right)
    1 teaspoon lemon juice
    ¼ teaspoon salt
    Few drops of Tabasco sauce
    2 tablespoons chopped onion
    1 can (7½ oz or 187 gm) crab meat,
      drained, flaked and cartilage removed
    15 small tomatoes

Blend together dressing, lemon juice, salt and Tabasco. Stir in crab meat. Halve, then hollow out tomatoes and stuff with crab mixture. Makes 30 appetizers.

Low-calorie Dressing

40-44 calories per tablespoon

    ¼ pint (125 ml) cider vinegar
    1 tablespoon tomato ketchup
    3 teaspoons Worcestershire sauce
    2 teaspoons Soy sauce
    1 clove garlic, crushed
    ¼ teaspoon dry mustard
    ¼ level teaspoon paprika
    Good shake each of salt and pepper
    Liquid artificial sweetener to taste

Put all the ingredients into a screw-topped jar and shake vigorously until well-blended. Use as required.

French Onion Soup

42 calories per serving

    1 large onion, thinly sliced
    1 oz (25 gm) butter or margarine
    2 cans condensed consommé
    ¼ pint (125 ml) water
    ½ teaspoon Worcestershire sauce
    Dash of pepper
    1 tablespoon grated Parmesan cheese

Cook onion in butter over medium-low heat till lightly browned, about 20 minutes. Add consommé, water and Worcestershire sauce. Bring to boil and season with pepper. Pour into bowls; sprinkle with Parmesan cheese. Serves 7.

Marinated Sprouts

13 calories per appetizer

    1 packet (10 oz or 250 gm) frozen
      Brussels sprouts
    ¼ pint (125 ml) low-calorie dressing (see
      above)
    2 tablespoons finely chopped onion
    1 teaspoon dried parsley
    ½ teaspoon dried dill

Cook Brussels sprouts according to directions on packet; drain. Cut large sprouts in half. Combine rest of ingredients and pour over warm Brussels sprouts. Cover and marinate in the refrigerator for several hours or overnight. Drain and serve with cocktail sticks. Serves 4-6.

Pickled Prawns

27 calories per appetizer

1 lb ($\frac{1}{2}$ kilo) fresh or frozen prawns in
  shells
1 medium celery stalk
2 tablespoons mixed pickling spices
1$\frac{1}{2}$ teaspoons salt
1 small onion, sliced
4 bay leaves
$\frac{1}{4}$ pint (125 ml) low-calorie dressing
  (page 8)
4 tablespoons white vinegar
1 tablespoon capers with liquid
1 teaspoon celery seed
$\frac{1}{2}$ teaspoon salt
Few drops of Tabasco sauce

Cover prawns with boiling water. Add celery, pickling spices and 1$\frac{1}{2}$ teaspoons salt. Cover and simmer for 5 minutes. Drain, peel and de-vein prawns under cold water. Mix with onion and bay leaves and arrange in a shallow dish. Combine remaining ingredients, mix well and pour over prawn mixture. Cover and marinate in the refrigerator for at least 24 hours, spooning marinade over prawns occasionally. Makes about 1 pint ($\frac{1}{2}$ litre). Serves 6.

Enjoy Marinated Sprouts as a snack between meals, or serve to your guests as a low-calorie hors d'oeuvre.

LOW-CALORIE

COOKING TIP

No need to serve high-calorie dips when appetizers, such as prawns, are marinated in low-calorie dressings. Spoon marinade over individual appetizers to develop full flavour.

Dill-flavoured Vegetable Sticks

89 calories per serving

1 lb ($\frac{1}{2}$ kilo) fresh green beans
1 lb ($\frac{1}{2}$ kilo) carrots
2 teaspoons dried dill
2 teaspoons mustard seed
4 cloves garlic, halved
1 pint ($\frac{1}{2}$ litre) water
$\frac{1}{4}$ pint (125 ml)+5 tablespoons vinegar
3 oz (75 gm) sugar

Cut ends from beans and wash thoroughly; leave whole. Cook in boiling, salted water for about 5 minutes, till crisp-tender. Drain. Peel carrots and cut into thin sticks. Cook in boiling, salted water till crisp-tender, about 3 minutes. Drain. Combine vegetables. Add dill, mustard seed and garlic. In a saucepan, combine water, vinegar and sugar. Bring to boil and pour over vegetables. Cool; cover and chill overnight. Vegetables may be stored for 2 weeks in the refrigerator. Serves 8.

Artichoke and Ham Bites

20 calories per appetizer

1 medium can artichoke hearts
$\frac{1}{4}$ pint (125 ml) low-calorie dressing
  (page 8)
$\frac{1}{8}$ teaspoon garlic powder
6 slices of boiled ham

Drain artichoke hearts and cut in half. Combine dressing and garlic powder; add artichokes. Marinate for several hours, then drain. Cut ham into strips, 4 inches by 1 inch. Wrap one strip around each artichoke half and secure with a wooden cocktail stick. Bake at Gas No 2 or 300°F (149°C) for about 10 minutes. Makes about 24 appetizers.

Halve eggs lengthwise; remove yolks. In a blender goblet combine yolks with rest of ingredients. Blend at medium speed till mixture is smooth, stopping blender to scrape sides occasionally. Spoon yolk mixture into egg whites; garnish with additional chopped parsley, if liked. Makes 12 appetizers.

Cheesy-herb Dip

22 calories per tablespoon

- 5 tablespoons low-calorie dressing (page 8)
- 3 oz (75 gm) curd cheese, softened
- 1 teaspoon mixed herbs
- ¼ teaspoon salt
- 1 tablespoon chopped parsley
- 1 tablespoon grated onion
- ½ teaspoon Worcestershire sauce
- 2 teaspoons capers, drained

Blend all ingredients and chill well. Serve as a dip for carrot sticks, celery sticks, and sliced cauliflowerets.

Tuna Balls

16 calories per appetizer

- 1 can (7½ oz or 187 gm) tuna, drained and flaked
- 3 oz (75 gm) curd cheese, softened
- 2 tablespoons finely chopped celery
- 2 teaspoons lemon juice
- ½ teaspoon Worcestershire sauce
- ¼ teaspoon salt
- 3 tablespoons finely chopped parsley

Blend tuna and cheese. Add celery, lemon juice, Worcestershire sauce and salt, then mix well. Allowing 2 teaspoons for each, form mixture into small balls. Roll in parsley. Chill well in the refrigerator. Serve on cocktail sticks. Makes about 30 appetizers.

Devilled Eggs

47 calories per appetizer

- 6 hard-boiled eggs
- 2 oz (50 gm) cottage cheese
- 2 tablespoons skimmed milk
- 1 tablespoon chopped parsley
- 1 teaspoon vinegar
- 1 teaspoon prepared mustard
- ¼ teaspoon salt
- ¼ teaspoon prepared horseradish
- Dash of pepper

Marrow Dip

25 calories per tablespoon

Serve with melba toast or vegetable sticks

- 1 small marrow, diced
- 1 tablespoon chopped onion
- ¼ pint (125 ml) tomato juice
- ½ teaspoon salt
- ⅛ teaspoon dried basil
- 8 oz (200 gm) curd cheese
- 1 tablespoon bacon, chopped and crisply fried

In a saucepan combine marrow, onion, tomato juice, salt and basil. Simmer, covered, for 20 minutes. Put in blender goblet with curd cheese. Cover and blend on high speed till mixture is smooth. Remove from blender and chill. Just before serving, stir in bacon. Makes just over ½ pint (250 ml).

LOW-CALORIE

COOKING TIP

Low-calorie dippers include vegetables, fruit and shellfish

Use natural yogurt, cottage cheese or curd cheese to save calories when making party dips.

Dieter's Dip

15 calories per tablespoon

12 oz (300 gm) cottage cheese
½ teaspoon mixed herbs
1 tablespoon finely chopped pimiento
1 tablespoon chopped parsley

Beat together well the cottage cheese and herbs. Stir in pimiento and parsley. Serve with chilled, cooked prawns. Makes about ½ pint (250 ml).

Party Cheese Dip

29 calories per tablespoon

Also delicious served as a salad dressing

5 oz (125 gm) curd cheese
1 tablespoon finely chopped pimiento
8 oz (200 gm) cottage cheese
3 tablespoons skimmed milk
1 teaspoon prepared horseradish
Several drops of Tabasco sauce

Combine all ingredients and beat till thoroughly blended and fluffy. Chill. Serve with raw vegetables or cooked prawns. Makes just under ¾ pint (375 ml).

Quick Fruit Dip

9 calories per tablespoon

½ pint (250 ml) natural yogurt
3 tablespoons diabetic jam
¼ teaspoon cinnamon

Combine yogurt, jam and cinnamon. Serve with dips of seedless grapes, apple slices sprinkled with lemon juice, cubes of melon and fresh pineapple pieces. Makes ½ pint (250 ml).

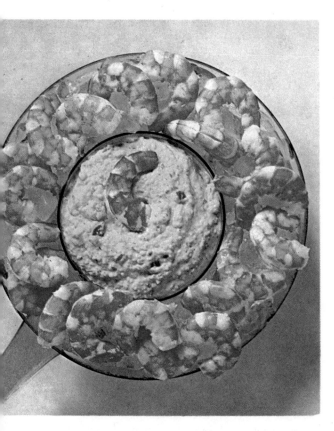

Even non-dieters will enjoy tempting Dieter's Dip made from cottage cheese and served with chilled, cooked prawns.

Scallops with Piquant Dip

20 calories per tablespoon

Chilled prawns may be substituted for scallops

12 oz (300 gm) scallops
2½ teaspoons salt
½ pint (250 ml) natural yogurt
3 tablespoons tomato ketchup
1 small pickled cucumber, finely chopped
½ teaspoon prepared mustard

Place scallops and 2 teaspoons salt in ¾ pint (375 ml) boiling water. Cover and return to boil. Reduce heat, then simmer for 3 to 4 minutes. Drain. Cut large scallops in half and chill thoroughly.

To prepare dip, combine yogurt with ketchup, cucumber, mustard and ½ teaspoon salt in a small bowl, and mix well. Chill and serve with chilled scallops. Makes ½ pint (250 ml).

Slimming Main Dishes

Stuffed Steak Rolls

252 calories per serving

6 flash fry or minute steaks
Salt and pepper
¼ pint (125 ml) low-calorie dressing
  (page 8)
3 medium carrots, grated
1 large onion, chopped
1 medium green pepper, chopped
2 medium celery stalks, chopped
5 tablespoons water
¼ pint (125 ml) beef stock
4 teaspoons cornflour
¼ teaspoon mixed herbs

Sprinkle steaks generously with salt and pepper, and brush with salad dressing. Place in a shallow dish, then marinate for 30 to 60 minutes at room temperature.

In a saucepan combine carrots, onion, green pepper, celery, 3 tablespoons water and ¼ teaspoon salt. Simmer, covered, till vegetables are crisp-tender, about 7 to 8 minutes. Drain.

Put equal amounts of vegetable mixture on to steaks. Roll up each like a Swiss roll and secure with cocktail sticks. Transfer to a large frying pan and pour beef stock over. Cover and simmer for 35 to 40 minutes or until tender. Transfer meat to a serving platter. Remove sticks. Skim off fat and reserve ¼ pint (125 ml) of stock. Blend cornflour with 2 tablespoons cold water and stir into reserved stock. Add mixed herbs and cook till mixture thickens. Pour over steak rolls. Serves 6.

LOW-CALORIE

COOKING TIP

*Grill or roast meat
to reduce main
dish calories*

Stand meat on a metal rack when grilling or roasting, to allow fat to escape. As the meat cooks, the fat slowly bastes and seasons the meat.

Devilled Steak

215 calories per serving

6 sirloin steaks, 1 inch thick
1½ oz (37 gm) butter or magarine
1 tablespoon chopped parsley
1 tablespoon dry sherry
1 teaspoon dry mustard
1 teaspoon Worcestershire sauce
¼ teaspoon salt
Dash of pepper
2 tablespoons warm brandy
3 tablespoons tomato ketchup
4 oz (100 gm) canned mushrooms

Trim excess fat from meat. Grill 3 inches from heat for 5 to 6 minutes on each side for rare steaks; longer for medium or well done. In a large frying pan combine butter and next six ingredients; heat till bubbly. Add steak and pour brandy over. Allow to flame. When flames have subsided, remove steak. Add ketchup and mushrooms to liquid in pan and mix well. Pour over steak. Serves 6.

Onion-smothered Steak

231 calories per serving

6 medium frying steaks, ¾ inch thick
3 level tablespoons flour
1 teaspoon salt
⅛ teaspoon pepper
2 tablespoons cooking fat
3 medium onions, sliced
½ pint (250 ml) water
1 tablespoon vinegar
1 clove garlic, chopped
1 bay leaf
¼ teaspoon thyme

Trim excess fat from meat. Combine flour, salt and pepper; coat steaks with flour mixture. Brown in hot cooking fat, then drain off excess fat. Top steaks with onions. Stir in water and remaining ingredients. Bring to boil, then reduce heat. Simmer, covered, for 1 hour. Remove bay leaf. Serves 6.

Oven-style Swiss Steak

171 calories per serving

2 lb (1 kilo) chuck steak, 1 inch thick
1 teaspoon salt
¼ teaspoon pepper
1 medium onion, sliced
1 can (4 oz or 100 gm) mushrooms, drained
½ pint (250 ml) home made or canned tomato sauce

Trim fat from meat. Pound meat with meat mallet and sprinkle with salt and pepper. Place meat in a baking dish, 1¾ inches deep and about 12 by 7 inches. Top with onion and mushrooms and pour sauce over. Cook, covered, at Gas No 4 or 350°F (177°C) for 2 hours. Uncover and cook for 15 minutes longer, basting occasionally. To serve, spoon sauce over meat. Serves 8.

Italian Veal Cutlets

250 calories per serving

4 boneless veal cutlets (1 lb or ½ kilo)
½ oz (12½ gm) cooking fat
1 can (8 oz or 200 gm) tomatoes, chopped
1 teaspoon Worcestershire sauce
1 tablespoon chopped parsley
2 teaspoons drained capers
¼ teaspoon garlic salt
¼ teaspoon oregano

Pound veal to ¼ inch thick or less. Brown quickly in hot fat. Blend remaining ingredients and add to meat. Cover and simmer for 35 to 40 minutes, then uncover and simmer till tender, about 10 minutes. To serve, spoon sauce over meat. Serves 4.

SEASONING GUIDE FOR MEATS

Spices and herbs add flavour to meat, fish and poultry without adding calories. Experiment with different seasonings by adding ¼ teaspoon dried herbs for each four servings. Increase the amount of herbs or spice if more seasoning is desired. To use dried herbs in leaf form, measure and then crush before adding to meat. To use fresh herbs, use three times more than the dried equivalent and chop, rather than crush. Use fresh herbs when available.

Beef	allspice, basil, bay leaf, caraway seed, celery seed, chilli powder, cumin, curry powder, dill, garlic, ginger, mace, marjoram, mustard, oregano, rosemary, savory, tarragon, thyme
Fish and Shellfish	basil, bay leaf, cardamom, celery seed, chilli powder, cumin, curry powder, dill, fennel, garlic, marjoram, mustard, oregano, paprika, rosemary, saffron, sage, savory, tarragon, thyme
Ham	allspice, cloves, cinnamon, coriander, curry powder, ginger, mustard
Lamb	allspice, basil, bay leaf, caraway seed, curry powder, dill, garlic, ginger, marjoram, mint, oregano, rosemary, sage, savory, thyme
Pork	basil, caraway seed, cloves, garlic, ginger, marjoram, mustard, nutmeg, oregano, paprika, rosemary, sage, savory, thyme
Poultry	basil, bay leaf, celery seed, chilli powder, cumin, curry powder, dill, garlic, ginger, marjoram, mustard, oregano, paprika, rosemary, saffron, sage, savory, tarragon, thyme
Veal	basil, bay leaf, curry powder, ginger, mace, marjoram, mint, mustard, oregano, rosemary, sage, savory, thyme

14

Green Pepper Steak

202 calories per serving

This can be served over rice

6 rump steaks, ½ inch thick
1 oz (25 gm) cooking fat
1 can (1 lb or ½ kilo) whole tomatoes
½ medium onion, thinly sliced
1 small clove garlic, chopped
2 teaspoons beef extract
1 teaspoon Worcestershire sauce
¼ teaspoon salt
Dash of pepper
2 medium green peppers, cut into ½ inch
  strips

Trim excess fat from steaks and cut into strips, 2 inches by ¼ inch. In a frying pan, brown meat strips in hot cooking fat. Drain off excess fat. Drain tomatoes, reserving liquid. Add reserved tomato liquid, onion slices, garlic, beef extract, Worcestershire sauce, salt and pepper to browned meat strips. Cover tightly and simmer mixture over low heat for 50 minutes. Stir in green pepper strips and drained tomatoes. Cook meat mixture, covered, till peppers are tender, about 6 to 8 minutes. Remove meat and vegetables to a serving bowl with a slotted spoon. Make up pan juices to ¼ pint (125 ml) with boiling water. Serve with the steak. Serves 6.

Meat dishes such as Devilled Steak and Onion-smothered Steak make calorie counting a pleasure. Serve them with a vegetable and a crisp, green salad.

Grilled Fillet Steaks

184 calories per serving

- ¼ pint (125 ml) dry red wine
- 2 tablespoons Soy sauce
- 1 medium onion, chopped
- 2 tablespoons finely chopped parsley
- 1 clove garlic, chopped
- Dash of pepper
- 4 fillet steaks, each 1 inch thick

Combine first six ingredients to make wine marinade. Place steaks in a plastic bag and pour marinade over them. Close bag and marinate for 2 hours in the refrigerator, pressing bag occasionally to distribute marinade. Remove steaks from bag and reserve marinade. Grill steaks 3 inches from heat for 7 minutes. Turn and grill 6 minutes longer or according to taste. Remove to a warm serving platter. Heat reserved marinade to boiling and spoon over grilled steaks. Serves 4.

Hawaiian Ham Slices

238 calories per serving

- 1 lb (½ kilo) cooked boneless ham
- 5 tablespoons pineapple juice
- 2 tablespoons Soy sauce
- ¾ teaspoon ground ginger
- 1 small clove garlic, chopped
- 4 canned pineapple rings

Trim excess fat from ham and slice into four equal-sized portions. Blend pineapple juice, Soy sauce, ground ginger and garlic. Pour over ham in a shallow container. Marinate for 30 minutes, turning once. Remove ham from marinade and stand under a pre-heated hot grill. Grill for 5 minutes, turn once and brush frequently with marinade. Heat pineapple rings under the grill during last 2 minutes. Top each slice of ham with a pineapple ring. Serves 4.

Highlight summer barbecues with Hawaiian Ham Slices. Before leaving home, marinate the ham in a piquant sauce. Then grill the ham and pineapple out of doors.

Frankfurter-sauerkraut Bake

212 calories per serving

1 lb (½ kilo) sauerkraut, drained
¼ pint (125 ml) mixed vegetable or
tomato juice
1 tablespoon chopped onion
1 dessertspoon mild mustard
8 frankfurters
1 medium green pepper, cut into thin
rings

In a 2 pint casserole combine sauerkraut, mixed vegetable or tomato juice, onion and mild mustard. Arrange frankfurters on top. Bake, covered, at Gas No 4 or 350°F (177°C) for 50 minutes. Top with thin rings of pepper. Bake, covered, for 10 minutes more. Serves 4.

Ham in Peach Sauce

217 calories per serving

4 gammon steaks
1 can (8 oz or 200 gm) diabetic peaches
1 dessertspoon cornflour
Pinch of ground cloves
½ teaspoon grated orange peel
4 tablespoons fresh orange juice

Trim excess fat from gammon steaks, and snip edges at 1 inch intervals. Stand in a grill pan, and grill 3 inches from heat for 7 to 8 minutes. Turn, and grill 5 to 6 minutes longer. Meanwhile, drain peaches, reserving 3 tablespoons liquid. Blend with cornflour and cloves. Add orange peel and juice. Cook, stirring, until mixture bubbles and thickens. Add peaches and heat through. Spoon on top of gammon steaks and serve at once. Serves 4.

London Grill

188 calories per serving

1 lb (½ kilo) rump steak slice, in one piece
¼ pint (125 ml) low-calorie dressing
(page 8)
1 dessertspoon lemon juice
1 level teaspoon finely grated lemon peel
Freshly milled pepper to taste
Salt

Score steak on both sides and stand in a shallow dish. Blend dressing with lemon juice, lemon peel and pepper. Pour over steak. Cover and leave at room temperature for 2 to 3 hours, turning frequently. Transfer to grill pan and grill 3 inches from heat for 5 minutes. Turn over and grill a further 5 to 6 minutes for medium rare steak. Season with salt. Carve steak into very thin slices diagonally across grain. Serves 4.

Pineapple-pork Chops

240 calories per serving

6 pork chops (2 lb or 1 kilo)
Salt and pepper
1 large can pineapple chunks
1 tablespoon brown sugar
1 medium onion, sliced
2 teaspoons cornflour
1 tablespoon cold water

Trim fat from chops and reserve trimmings. In a frying pan heat trimmings till 1 tablespoon fat accumulates; discard trimmings. Brown chops on both sides in hot fat; drain and season. Drain pineapple chunks, reserving ¼ pint (125 ml) syrup. Mix with brown sugar, onion and the pineapple chunks. Return chops to the pan and arrange onion and pineapple mixture on top. Cover and simmer for 45 minutes, then transfer chops to a warm serving dish. Skim off fat from pan. Blend cornflour with cold water and stir into pan. Cook, stirring, until thick and bubbly. Spoon over chops. Serves 6.

Orange-glazed Lamb

350 calories per serving

8 lamb loin chops, ¾ inch thick
Salt
3 tablespoons diabetic orange marmalade
2 teaspoons lemon juice
Orange slices (optional)

Trim excess fat from lamb chops and season with salt. Grill 3 to 4 inches from heat for 6 to 8 minutes. Turn and grill 4 minutes more. Combine marmalade and lemon juice, and spread over chops. Grill till done, about 4 to 6 minutes more. Garnish with orange slices, heated for a few minutes, if liked. Serves 4.

Low-calorie marinades add flavour to meat. Pour marinade over meat in plastic bag and close. Press bag to distribute marinade.

Barbecued Rump Steak

291 calories per serving

1½ lb (¾ kilo) piece of rump steak
4 tablespoons wine vinegar
3 tablespoons tomato ketchup
2 tablespoons Soy sauce
1 teaspoon salt
2 teaspoons Worcestershire sauce
1 teaspoon prepared mustard
¼ teaspoon garlic powder
¼ teaspoon pepper

Remove fat from steak and place meat in a plastic bag set in a deep bowl. Mix vinegar, ketchup, Soy sauce, salt, Worcestershire sauce, mustard, garlic powder and pepper. Pour over meat and close bag. Marinate for 2 to 3 hours at room temperature or overnight in the refrigerator. Turn bag occasionally to distribute marinade. Remove meat from bag and reserve marinade. Place meat in grill pan. Grill for 15 to 20 minutes, turning twice and basting frequently with marinade. Serves 4.

Liver with Mushrooms

181 calories per serving

4 oz (100 gm) mushrooms, sliced
4 tablespoons low-calorie dressing
    (page 8)
1 lb (½ kilo) calves liver

Marinate mushrooms in dressing for 30 minutes. Meanwhile, cut liver into serving-sized pieces and brush all over with dressing. Stand in grill pan and grill 3 inches from heat for 4 minutes. Turn, then top liver with mushrooms. Grill a further 4 minutes. Serves 4.

Marinated Pot Roast

260 calories per serving

3 lb (1½ kilo) piece of chuck steak
½ pint (250 ml) pineapple juice
¼ pint (125 ml) wine vinegar
1 medium onion, sliced
1 clove garlic, chopped
2 bay leaves
2 teaspoons Worcestershire sauce
¼ pint (125 ml) water
2 teaspoons salt
¼ teaspoon pepper
3 tablespoons flour
3 tablespoons cold water

Trim excess fat from meat, place meat in a plastic bag and set in a deep bowl. Mix juice and all remaining ingredients except flour and 3 tablespoons water. Pour over meat and close bag. Marinate overnight in the refrigerator, occasionally turning bag to distribute marinade.

Next day, transfer meat from the bag to a casserole. Strain marinade and reserve ½ pint (250 ml) liquid. Add strained onion, bay leaves and reserved liquid to meat. Cover tightly and simmer for 2¼ to 2½ hours. Remove meat. Skim fat from pan juices, reserving ½ pint (250 ml) juices. Remove bay leaves. Mix flour with 3 tablespoons cold water and add to reserved juices. Cook and stir till bubbly, and continue to cook for 2 to 3 minutes more. Spoon over meat. Serves 8.

A Sunday lunch treat for slimmers—Marinated Pot Roast with its tangy, spicy sauce.

Fruited Chicken Breasts

157 calories per serving

3 large chicken breasts (2 lb or 1 kilo)
Salt
1 chicken stock cube
½ pint (250 ml) boiling water
¼ teaspoon grated orange peel
3 tablespoons fresh orange juice
1 tablespoon finely chopped onion
Dash of pepper
1 tablespoon cornflour
2 tablespoons cold water
1 teacup halved and de-seeded grapes
Paprika
1 medium orange, sliced

Cut chicken breasts in halves lengthwise. Sprinkle with salt. Arrange chicken in a baking dish, 1¾ inches deep and about 10 by 6 inches. Dissolve the stock cube in ½ pint (250 ml) boiling water. Stir in orange peel and juice, onion and a dash of pepper, then pour over chicken. Cover with foil and bake at Gas No 4 or 350°F (177°C) for 50 to 60 minutes or until tender. Remove chicken to a warm serving platter. Strain pan juices, reserving 1 teacup for sauce. In a saucepan, blend cornflour with 2 tablespoons cold water and stir in reserved pan juices. Cook, stirring constantly, until mixture is thick and bubbly. Cook a further minute. Stir in grapes and heat through. Spoon sauce over chicken and sprinkle with paprika. Garnish with orange slices and serve immediately. Serves 6.

Grilled Chicken is a favourite all the year round. Prepare it indoors or grill outside over a barbecue. Brush with glaze to improve browning and flavour.

Curried Chicken

249 calories per serving

$\frac{1}{4}$ pint (125 ml) water
$\frac{3}{4}$ pint (375 ml) canned vegetable or
  tomato juice
1 chicken stock cube, crumbled
2 lb (1 kilo) roasting chicken, cut up and
  skinned
1 medium onion, chopped
1 teaspoon curry powder
$\frac{1}{2}$ teaspoon poultry seasoning
$\frac{1}{2}$ teaspoon salt
Dash of pepper
1 tablespoon flour
1 small can unsweetened grapefruit
  sections, drained

In a frying pan, combine water, the same amount ($\frac{1}{4}$ pint or 125 ml) of canned vegetable or tomato juice and stock cube. Add chicken, onion, curry powder, poultry seasoning, salt and pepper. Simmer, covered, for 45 minutes. Remove chicken and skim off fat. Blend $\frac{1}{2}$ pint (250 ml) additional vegetable or tomato juice with flour and add to pan. Cook, stirring, till thick and bubbly. Return chicken to sauce, and top with unsweetened grapefruit sections. Cover and heat through. Serves 4.

Grilled Chicken

271 calories per serving

An ideal dish for a barbecue

$\frac{1}{4}$ pint (125 ml) low-calorie dressing
  (page 8)
3 tablespoons Soy sauce
1 small onion, chopped
1 teaspoon dry mustard
3 spring or baby chickens, each 1$\frac{1}{2}$ lb or
  $\frac{3}{4}$ kilo

Blend dressing, Soy sauce, onion and mustard. Halve and skin chickens and stand in a grill pan. Brush heavily with Soy mixture. Grill 5 to 7 inches from heat for 20 minutes, brushing occasionally with Soy mixture. Turn and brush with Soy mixture. Grill for a further 20 minutes. Serves 6.

    To grill outside, cook chicken over medium coals till lightly browned, about 20 minutes; brush occasionally with mixture. Turn and grill till tender, 15 to 20 minutes, brushing occasionally.

LOW-CALORIE

COOKING TIP

Remove skin from poultry to reduce calories

Skinning poultry removes about 40 calories per serving. One 3$\frac{1}{2}$ oz (87 gm) serving of light meat, skinned, provides 197 calories compared to an equal serving of light meat, unskinned, which contains 234 calories. A serving of light meat also has about 20 calories less than the same amount of dark meat.

Grilled Chicken Worcestershire

271 calories per serving

Follow the recipe for Grilled Chicken, but brush chicken with approximately 2 tablespoons Worcestershire sauce and 1 tablespoon lemon juice beaten with 1 tablespoon tomato ketchup and seasoned well with garlic, salt and pepper. For a novelty garnish, accompany with wedges of unpeeled orange.

Chicken in Tomato Sauce

151 calories per serving

This recipe adds flavour to frozen chicken

3 large or 6 small chicken breasts,
  skinned and boned
1 teaspoon seasoned salt
Dash of paprika
1 can (1 lb or $\frac{1}{2}$ kilo) tomatoes
1 medium onion, thinly sliced and
  separated into rings
4 oz (100 gm) mushrooms, sliced
2 tablespoons chopped parsley
$\frac{1}{2}$ teaspoon oregano
$\frac{1}{2}$ teaspoon celery seed
1 clove garlic, chopped
1 bay leaf

Place chicken breasts in a baking dish, 1$\frac{3}{4}$ inches deep and about 12 by 7 inches; sprinkle with salt and paprika. Drain tomatoes, reserving 3 tablespoons liquid. Arrange tomatoes, onion and mushrooms over chicken. Sprinkle parsley, oregano and celery seed on top. Mix reserved liquid, garlic and bay leaf, and pour over chicken. Cover and bake at Gas No 4 or 350°F (177°C) for 1 hour. Uncover, and bake 10 minutes more. Remove bay leaf, and spoon juices over chicken. Serves 6.

LOW-CALORIE

COOKING TIP

Make white sauce with little or no fat

Blend flour with a small amount of cold skimmed milk. Stir into remaining milk and fat (if used). Cook and stir till bubbly. For rich colour, add a few drops of yellow food colouring.

Frankfurters and Sauerkraut

135 calories per serving

4 frankfurters
1 lb (½ kilo) sauerkraut
½ teaspoon caraway seeds
2 oz (50 gm) grated Gruyère cheese

Slice frankfurters diagonally into ½ inch pieces and brown in a frying pan. Add undrained sauerkraut and caraway seeds. Cook, stirring, over medium heat till most of the liquid has evaporated. Stir in cheese and heat until melted, about 2 to 3 minutes. Serves 4.

Turkey Hawaiian

310 calories per serving

1 can (1 lb or ½ kilo) pineapple slices
1 can condensed consommé
1 packet (10 oz or 250 gm) frozen peas
2 oz (50 gm) mushrooms, sliced
4 celery stalks, bias-cut into ¼ inch slices
1 small onion, chopped
3 tablespoons Soy sauce
3 tablespoons cornflour
3 tablespoons cold water
12 oz (300 gm) turkey, cooked and diced
1 can (5 oz or 125 gm) water chestnuts, drained and sliced
8 oz (200 gm) cooked rice

Drain pineapple, reserving syrup. Make up syrup to ½ pint (250 ml) with water. Put into saucepan. Add consommé, peas, mushrooms, celery, onion and Soy sauce; bring to boil. Cover and simmer for 5 minutes. Blend cornflour with cold water, and add to saucepan. Cook, stirring, until thickened and bubbly. Cut up pineapple and stir into saucepan with turkey and water chestnuts; heat through. Serve over hot cooked rice. Serves 8.

Basic Meat Loaf

271 calories per serving

An ideal cold dish for a picnic

1 beef stock cube
3 tablespoons boiling water
1 egg, beaten
3 oz (75 gm) fresh white breadcrumbs
1 small onion, chopped
½ teaspoon sage
¼ teaspoon salt
Dash of pepper
1 lb (½ kilo) lean minced beef
3 tablespoons Tabasco or chilli sauce

Dissolve stock cube in boiling water. Mix with egg, breadcrumbs, onion, sage, salt and pepper. Add beef and mix well. Shape into a loaf in a shallow baking dish. Bake at Gas No 4 or 350°F (177°C) for 45 minutes. Spread sauce over loaf, then bake 10 to 15 minutes more. Serves 4.

Stuffed Peppers

212 calories per serving

Low in calories when stuffed with meat

8 medium green peppers
Salt
1 lb (½ kilo) lean minced beef
1 small onion, chopped
2 slices toast, cubed
4 oz (100 gm) Mozzarella cheese, shredded
2 oz (50 gm) mushrooms, sliced
2 medium tomatoes, skinned and chopped
½ teaspoon Worcestershire sauce

Cut tops off green peppers, and remove seeds and membrane. Pre-cook in boiling, salted water for 5 minutes; drain. (For crisper peppers, omit pre-cooking.) Generously sprinkle inside of peppers with salt. In a frying pan, brown (dry fry) beef with onion. Stir in toast, 2 oz (50 gm) Mozzarella cheese, mushrooms, tomatoes, Worcestershire sauce and ½ teaspoon salt. Spoon into peppers. Place in a baking dish, 1¾ inches deep and about 10 by 6 inches. Bake, covered, at Gas No 4 or 350°F (177°C) for 25 minutes. Uncover, and sprinkle with 2 oz (50 gm) Mozzarella cheese. Bake for 5 to 10 minutes more. Serves 8.

Vegetable and Cod Bake

111 calories per serving

4 portions cod fillet (1 lb or ½ kilo)
3 tablespoons lemon juice
1 teaspoon salt
½ teaspoon paprika
4 oz (100 gm) mushrooms, sliced
1 large tomato, skinned and chopped
½ medium green pepper, chopped
1 tablespoon chopped parsley
Lemon wedges

Place cod fillets in a greased baking dish, 1¾ inches deep and about 10 by 6 inches. Sprinkle with lemon juice, salt and paprika. Combine mushrooms, tomato, green pepper and parsley, and sprinkle over fish. Bake, covered, at Gas No 4 or 350°F (177°C) till fish flakes easily with a fork, about 25 minutes. Serve with lemon wedges. Serves 4.

Foil-baked Halibut

139 calories per serving

4 slices of halibut (1 lb or ½ kilo)
1 teaspoon salt
Pepper
Paprika
4 teaspoons lemon juice
2 carrots, cut into strips
1 small green pepper, cut into rings
1 medium onion, sliced

Tear off four lengths of kitchen foil and centre a fish slice on each piece of foil. Sprinkle each with ¼ teaspoon salt, dash of pepper, dash of paprika and 1 teaspoon lemon juice. Put equal amounts of vegetables on to each slice of fish. Draw up four corners of foil to the centre and twist securely. Bake at Gas No 8 or 450°F (232°C) till fish flakes easily with a fork, about 25 minutes. Serves 4.

Salmon Dolmas

216 calories per serving

1 egg, beaten
1 small onion, chopped
¼ teaspoon salt
Dash of pepper

1 teaspoon Worcestershire sauce
1 can (1 lb or ½ kilo) pink salmon, drained, flaked and bones removed
3 oz (75 gm) cooked rice
6 large cabbage leaves
Paprika

CHEESE SAUCE:
1 oz (25 gm) butter or margarine
1 oz (25 gm) flour
½ pint (250 ml) skimmed milk
¼ teaspoon salt
Dash of pepper
2 oz (50 gm) Cheddar cheese, grated
1 tablespoon lemon juice

Combine first five ingredients. Add salmon and rice and mix well. Immerse cabbage in boiling water till limp, 2 to 3 minutes, and drain. Split heavy centre vein of cabbage for 2 inches up leaf. Put equal amounts of salmon mixture on each leaf. Fold in sides and tuck ends underneath. Place in a shallow baking dish and cover with foil. Bake at Gas No 4 or 350°F (177°C) for 45 minutes. Serve with cheese sauce, and garnish with paprika. Serves 6.

Cheese Sauce: melt butter or margarine, blend in flour and add milk, salt and pepper. Cook, stirring, till thick and bubbly. Remove sauce from heat; add cheese and lemon juice. Stir until cheese melts.

Lemon and Haddock Bake

106 calories per serving

2 packets (each 1 lb or ½ kilo) frozen haddock fillets or 2 lb (1 kilo) fresh haddock fillets
½ teaspoon salt
4 oz (100 gm) mushrooms, sliced
1 small onion, chopped
½ green pepper, chopped
8 thin lemon slices
4 tablespoons dry white wine or cider
Paprika

Thaw haddock fillets, if frozen, and cut into eight portions. Place in a greased baking dish, 1¾ inches deep and about 12 by 7 inches. Sprinkle with salt, and top with mushrooms, onion, green pepper and lemon slices. Pour white wine or cider over fish and sprinkle with paprika. Cover and bake at Gas No 4 or 350°F (177°C) till fish flakes, about 30 minutes. Serves 8.

Use grapefruit to enhance the flavour of fish

Grapefruit adds a distinctive piquancy to white fish. Sprinkle fish with grapefruit juice while grilling; garnish with segments of fresh grapefruit before serving.

Orange-halibut Fillets

142 calories per serving

- 4 portions haddock fillet (1 lb or ½ kilo)
- 2 tablespoons thawed orange juice concentrate
- 1 tablespoon chopped parsley
- 1 tablespoon lemon juice
- ½ teaspoon dried dill
- ¼ pint (125 ml) water
- ¼ teaspoon salt
- 4 thin orange slices

Place fish in shallow pan. Mix concentrate and next five ingredients, and pour over fish. Marinate for 30 minutes, turning once. Remove fish, reserving marinade. Place fish in a well-greased grill pan. Grill 3 inches from heat for 6 minutes. Turn and grill till fish flakes easily with a fork, about 5 to 6 minutes. Baste with reserved marinade. To serve, brush with marinade and top with orange slices. Serves 4.

Fish with Italian Sauce

149 calories per serving

- 8 fillets of haddock (2 lb or 1 kilo)
- Salt
- 1 can (8 oz or 200 gm) Italian style tomato sauce
- 2 tablespoons chopped onion
- 4 oz (100 gm) Mozzarella cheese, shredded

Arrange fillets in a single layer on a well-greased baking sheet, 1 inch deep and about 15 by 10 inches. Sprinkle with salt. Mix sauce and onion, and pour over fillets. Bake, uncovered, at Gas No 4 or 350°F (177°C) till fish flakes easily with a fork, about 25 to 30 minutes. Sprinkle with cheese and return to oven till cheese melts, about 3 minutes. Serves 8.

Fish with Italian Sauce has a tomato-cheese topping similar to pizza, but without the calories.

Seafood Divan

115 calories per serving

Not cheap, but delicious all the same

- 2 packets (each 10 oz or 250 gm) frozen broccoli spears
- 5 oz (125 gm) canned crab meat, flaked
- 4 oz (100 gm) peeled prawns
- ½ pint (250 ml)+3 tablespoons skimmed milk
- 2 tablespoons flour
- ¼ teaspoon salt
- 1 oz (25 gm) butter
- 2 oz (50 gm) Cheddar cheese, grated
- Paprika

Cook broccoli spears, following directions on the packet, then drain. Arrange in a greased baking dish, 1¾ inches deep and about 12 by 7 inches. Mix crab meat with prawns and spoon over broccoli. In a blender goblet combine 3 tablespoons skimmed milk, flour and salt. Blend well, then pour into saucepan. Add ½ pint (250 ml) skimmed milk and the butter. Cook, stirring, until thick, then add Cheddar cheese. Stir until cheese has melted. Pour over fish, covering it completely. Sprinkle with paprika. Bake at Gas No 6 or 400°F (204°C) for 20 to 25 minutes. Serves 8.

Sweet and Sour Prawns

187 calories per serving

- 1 can (1 lb or ½ kilo) pineapple chunks
- 1 medium green pepper, cut into strips
- 1 small onion, sliced
- 1 teaspoon yeast extract
- 2 tablespoons brown sugar
- 4 teaspoons cornflour
- 1 tablespoon cold water
- 2 teaspoons vinegar
- 8 oz (200 gm) peeled prawns

Drain pineapple chunks. Reserve syrup and make up to ½ pint (250 ml) with water. Cut up pineapple. In a saucepan combine juice mixture, pineapple, green pepper, onion and yeast extract. Bring to boil and simmer, covered, for 3 to 4 minutes. Blend brown sugar, cornflour, water and vinegar, and add to pineapple mixture. Cook, stirring, till thick and bubbly. Fold in prawns and heat through. Serves 6.

To make a plain omelette, lightly brush a non-stick shallow pan with salad oil before cooking. Pour omelette mixture into pan and cook. Using a spatula, mark omelette in thirds with two shallow parallel cuts.

Puffy Omelette

103 calories per serving

4 eggs, separated
2 tablespoons water
¼ teaspoon salt
1 oz (25 gm) butter or margarine

Beat egg whites till frothy, then add water and salt and beat till stiff peaks form. Beat egg yolks till thick and lemon-coloured. Fold yolks into whites. Melt butter in a 10 inch ovenproof frying pan and heat till a drop of water sizzles. Pour in omelette mixture and spread to edges of pan, leaving sides higher. Reduce heat and cook till puffed and the bottom is golden, about 8 minutes. Then bake at Gas No 3 or 325°F (163°C) for about 8 to 10 minutes or brown at least 3 inches below a pre-heated grill, till a knife inserted in the centre of the omelette comes out clean. Loosen sides of omelette, and make a shallow, off-centre cut across it. Tilt pan; fold smaller portion over larger portion. Slip on to a platter and serve immediately. Serves 4.

Macaroni-cheese Puff

226 calories per serving

2 oz (50 gm) elbow macaroni
½ pint (250 ml)+3 tablespoons skimmed milk
6 oz (150 gm) strong Cheddar cheese, grated
¼ teaspoon salt
3 eggs, separated
2 oz (50 gm) fresh white breadcrumbs
3 tablespoons chopped canned pimiento
2 tablespoons chopped onion
¼ teaspoon cream of tartar

Cook macaroni in boiling, salted water till tender; drain. Combine milk, cheese and salt, and stir over low heat till cheese melts. Stir a small amount of hot mixture into beaten egg yolks. Return to hot mixture in pan and blend well. Stir in macaroni, breadcrumbs, pimiento and onion. Beat egg whites with cream of tartar till stiff. Fold into macaroni mixture. Pour into an ungreased 2 pint (1½ litre) soufflé dish. Bake at Gas No 3 or 325°F (163°C) for about 1 hour, till a knife, inserted off-centre, comes out clean. Serve immediately. Serves 6.

Tomato and Egg Scramble

136 calories per serving

6 eggs
3 tablespoons skimmed milk
½ teaspoon salt
¼ teaspoon dried oregano
¼ teaspoon dried parsley flakes
Dash of pepper
8 oz (200 gm) tomatoes, skinned and chopped

With a fork beat together eggs, skimmed milk, salt, oregano, parsley flakes and pepper. Pour into a warm non-stick pan. Cook over low heat, lifting mixture from bottom of the pan with a spatula. When nearly done, fold in tomatoes. Serve immediately. Serves 4.

To remove omelette from pan, tilt pan. Gently fold each side of omelette over centre portion, envelope-style. Carefully slip folded omelette on to a warm serving platter.

Prawn and Mushroom Soufflé

202 calories per serving

2 tablespoons softened butter or
  margarine
3 tablespoons flour
½ teaspoon salt
Dash of pepper
¼ pint (125 ml)+4 tablespoons skimmed
  milk
4 eggs, separated
4 oz (100 gm) peeled prawns
2 oz (50 gm) canned mushrooms, drained
  and chopped
2 tablespoons chopped parsley

In a saucepan melt butter, then blend in flour, salt and pepper. Add milk and cook, stirring, till thick and bubbly. Remove from heat. Beat egg yolks till thick and lemon-coloured. Slowly add to white sauce, stirring constantly. Stir in prawns, mushrooms and parsley. Beat egg whites to stiff peaks. Gradually pour prawn mixture over egg whites, folding together thoroughly. Turn into an ungreased 2 pint (1¼ litre) soufflé dish. Bake at Gas No 4 or 350°F (177°C) till a knife inserted off-centre comes out clean, about 45 minutes. Serve immediately. Serves 4.

Chicken and Lemon Soufflé

203 calories per serving

2 tablespoons softened butter or
  margarine
3 tablespoons flour
½ teaspoon salt
Dash of pepper
¼ pint (125 ml)+4 tablespoons skimmed
  milk
4 eggs, separated
3 oz (75 gm) chicken breast, skinned,
  cooked and finely minced
1 teaspoon finely grated lemon peel

In a saucepan melt butter, then blend in flour, salt and pepper. Add milk, and cook, stirring, till thick and bubbly. Remove from heat. Beat egg yolks until thick and lemon-coloured. Slowly add to white sauce, stirring constantly. Stir in chicken and lemon peel. Beat egg whites to stiff peaks. Gradually pour chicken mixture over egg whites, folding together thoroughly. Turn into an un-greased 2 pint (1¼ litre) soufflé dish. Bake exactly as directed for Prawn and Mushroom Soufflé (see left). Serves 4.

Cheese Soufflé

273 calories per serving

2 tablespoons softened butter or
  margarine
3 tablespoons flour
½ teaspoon salt
Dash of cayenne pepper
¼ pint (125 ml)+4 tablespoons skimmed
  milk
4 oz (100 gm) processed cheese, grated
4 eggs, separated

In a saucepan melt butter and blend in flour, salt and cayenne. Add skimmed milk; cook and stir till thick and bubbly. Remove from heat. Add cheese and stir till melted. Beat egg yolks till thick and lemon-coloured. Add cheese mixture, stirring constantly, and cool slightly. Beat egg whites to stiff peaks. Pour yolk mixture over whites, folding together thoroughly. Pour into ungreased 2 pint (1¼ litre) soufflé dish. For a top that puffs in the oven, trace a circle through mixture 1 inch from edge and 1 inch deep. Bake at Gas No 4 or 350°F (177°C) till a knife inserted off-centre comes out clean, about 45 minutes. Serve immediately. Serves 4.

Mushroom Omelette

123 calories per serving

3 eggs
1 tablespoon water
¼ teaspoon salt
Dash of pepper
Dash of mixed herbs
2 oz (50 gm) canned mushrooms, sliced,
  heated and drained

With a fork beat eggs, water, salt, pepper and herbs till blended but not frothy. Lightly brush an 8 inch pan with salad oil, and heat. Add eggs and cook slowly. Run spatula around edges and lift to allow uncooked portion to flow underneath. Cook till set but still shiny. Remove from heat, then spoon mushrooms down centre of omelette. With a spatula, fold omelette in three, envelope-style. Tilt pan; slip on to platter. Serves 2.

Calorie-lean Vegetables

Cauliflower Italiano

35 calories per serving

- 1 tablespoon chopped onion
- 1 small clove garlic, crushed
- 2 tablespoons low-calorie dressing (page 8)
- 1 medium sized cauliflower, divided into florets
- 3 tablespoons water
- 2 tablespoons chopped green pepper
- 8 small tomatoes, halved
- ½ teaspoon salt
- ⅛ teaspoon dried basil

In an 8 inch frying pan cook onion and garlic in salad dressing till tender; add cauliflower and 3 tablespoons water. Cook, covered, over low heat for 10 minutes. Add green pepper, and cook till cauliflower is tender, about 5 minutes. Stir in remaining ingredients, and heat through. Serves 6.

Asparagus with Cheese

78 calories per serving

- 1 lb (½ kilo) fresh asparagus spears or 1 packet (10 oz or 250 gm) frozen asparagus spears
- 2 oz (50 gm) processed cheese, grated
- 2 tablespoons chopped canned pimiento
- 2 teaspoons sesame seed, toasted

In a 10 inch frying pan cook asparagus spears in boiling, salted water till tender, and drain. Toss together cheese, pimiento, and sesame seed, and sprinkle over spears. Stand under a hot grill just long enough for cheese to melt. Serves 4.

Enticing vegetable dishes, such as Cauliflower Italiano and Asparagus with Cheese, offer low-calorie eating at its best.

Apple-flavoured Beetroot

61 calories per serving

- 2 teaspoons cornflour
- 2 teaspoons sugar
- Dash of salt
- ¼ pint (125 ml) apple juice
- 1 lb (½ kilo) cooked beetroot, sliced
- ¼ teaspoon shredded orange peel

In a saucepan blend cornflour, sugar and salt. Stir in apple juice, and cook, stirring, over medium heat till thickened and bubbly. Add beetroot and orange peel. Simmer, uncovered, for 10 minutes. Serves 4.

Oriental Spinach

25 calories per serving

- 1 packet (10 oz or 250 gm) frozen spinach, chopped
- 1 can (1 lb or ½ kilo) bean sprouts, drained and rinsed
- 1 can (5 oz or 125 gm) water chestnuts, drained and sliced
- 4 teaspoons Soy sauce

Cook spinach following packet directions but do not drain. Stir in bean sprouts and water chestnuts. Bring to boil and drain. Toss with Soy sauce. Serve piping hot. Serves 8.

Basil Carrots

39 calories per serving

- 6 medium carrots
- 1 tablespoon melted butter
- ¼ teaspoon salt
- ¼ teaspoon dried basil

Slice carrots and simmer, covered, in salted water till tender, about 10 to 15 minutes, then drain. Combine butter, salt and basil and toss with carrots. Serves 6.

Broccoli and Tomato Stack-ups

68 calories per serving

1 packet (10 oz or 250 gm) frozen
  broccoli, chopped
3 large tomatoes
Salt
2 oz (50 gm) processed cheese, grated
2 tablespoons chopped onion

Cook broccoli according to packet directions; drain. Cut each tomato into four slices. Sprinkle tomato slices with salt, and place on a baking sheet. Combine broccoli, 2 tablespoons of the cheese, and onion. Spoon broccoli mixture over tomato slices. Grill 4 to 5 inches from heat for 10 to 12 minutes. Sprinkle with remaining cheese. Return to grill for about 1 to 2 minutes. Serves 6.

Herbed Tomato Halves

56 calories per serving

3 medium tomatoes, cut in half crosswise
Salt
1 oz (25 gm) fresh white breadcrumbs
1 tablespoon melted butter
$\frac{1}{4}$ teaspoon basil
2 tablespoons grated Parmesan cheese

Arrange tomato halves in a baking dish, $1\frac{3}{4}$ inches deep and about 10 by 6 inches. Sprinkle with salt. Toss breadcrumbs with melted butter, basil and cheese. Sprinkle on tomato halves. Bake, uncovered, at Gas No 4 or 350°F (177°C) for 20 to 25 minutes. Serves 6.

SEASONING GUIDE FOR VEGETABLES

Spices and herbs add appeal without adding calories. Add seasoning to vegetables as they cook or lightly sprinkle over food before serving. Begin with $\frac{1}{4}$ teaspoon dried herbs for each four servings and increase until desired flavour level is reached. To use dried herbs in leaf form, measure and then crush before adding to vegetables. To use fresh herbs, use three times more of the seasoning and chop, rather than crush. Use fresh herbs when available.

Artichoke	bay leaf, marjoram, thyme
Asparagus	caraway seed, mustard, nutmeg, sesame seed, tarragon
Aubergine	allspice, bay leaf, chilli powder, marjoram
Beans, green	basil, dill, marjoram, mustard, nutmeg, oregano, savory, thyme
Beetroot	allspice, bay leaf, caraway seed, cloves, ginger, mustard
Broccoli	caraway seed, mustard, oregano, tarragon
Brussels sprouts	caraway seed, mustard, nutmeg, sage
Cabbage	caraway seed, celery seed, cumin, curry powder, fennel, mustard
Carrots	allspice, bay leaf, cinnamon, curry powder, dill, ginger, nutmeg
Cauliflower	cayenne, celery seed, chilli powder, nutmeg, paprika, rosemary
Marrow	allspice, bay leaf, cinnamon, cloves, ginger, nutmeg, paprika
Onions	bay leaf, mustard, oregano, paprika, sage
Peas	chilli powder, dill, oregano, poppy seed, rosemary, sage
Potatoes	caraway seed, fennel, mustard, oregano, paprika, sesame seed
Spinach	allspice, cinnamon, nutmeg, oregano, rosemary, sesame seed
Sweet corn	cayenne, celery seed, chilli powder, curry powder, paprika
Sweet potatoes	cardamom seed, cinnamon, cloves, nutmeg, poppy seed
Tomatoes	basil, celery seed, chilli powder, curry powder, oregano
Turnips	allspice, celery seed, curry powder, dill, oregano

Sesame Broccoli

74 calories per serving

  1 lb (½ kilo) fresh broccoli
  1 tablespoon salad oil
  1 tablespoon vinegar
  1 tablespoon Soy sauce
  4 teaspoons sugar
  1 tablespoon sesame seed, toasted

Cook broccoli in a small amount of boiling, salted water till tender, about 15 minutes, then drain. In a saucepan combine rest of the ingredients. Heat to boiling. Pour over broccoli, and turn to coat. Serves 5.

*Vegetable cooking
methods should add
flavour, not calories*

Waterless cooking allows fresh vegetables to cook in their own natural juices. Vegetables are cooked over low to medium heat with little or no liquid added. Seasonings may be added to vegetables before or after cooking.

Green Beans with Onions, above right, make a delectable combination with a pinch of marjoram. Sesame Broccoli, below, with sweet-sour sauce topped with sesame seeds, makes an unusual vegetable.

Green Beans with Onions

61 calories per serving

  1 packet (9 oz or 225 gm) frozen cut
    green beans
  ½ teaspoon marjoram
  4 small onions, boiled
  ½ oz (12 gm) butter or margarine

Cook beans according to packet directions, but add marjoram to cooking liquid. Halve onions lengthwise, and add to beans during last few minutes of cooking time. Continue cooking till onions are heated through. Drain thoroughly and stir in butter or margarine. Turn vegetables into serving dish. Serves 4.

Peas with Mushrooms

38 calories per serving

  1 packet (10 oz or 250 gm) frozen peas
  4 oz (100 gm) mushrooms, sliced
  1 teaspoon lemon juice
  ¼ teaspoon basil
  Salt and pepper

Cook peas according to packet directions but do not drain. Add mushrooms and heat through. Drain. Add lemon juice and basil, and season with salt and pepper. Serves 6.

Cheesy Onion Slices

42 calories per serving

3 tablespoons low-calorie dressing
  (page 8)
4 tablespoons water
½ teaspoon salt
3 large onions, cut into ½ inch slices
2 tablespoons chopped parsley
2 tablespoons grated Parmesan cheese
Paprika

In a frying pan heat dressing, water and salt.
Place onion slices in a single layer in the frying
pan. Cover, and cook over low heat for 10
minutes. Turn, and sprinkle with parsley, cheese
and paprika. Cook, covered, for 5 minutes more.
Serves 6.

Baked Stuffed Potatoes

60 calories per serving

3 medium baking potatoes
4 tablespoons hot water
3 tablespoons instant low-fat milk
  granules
½ teaspoon salt
Dash of pepper
Paprika

Scrub potatoes and puncture skin with a fork.
Bake at Gas No 7 or 425°F (218°C) for 1 hour.
Cut potatoes in half lengthwise. Scoop out inside
and mash. Combine water, milk powder, salt and
pepper. Add to potatoes and heat till fluffy, adding
some more hot water if needed. Pile lightly into
reserved potato shells and sprinkle with paprika.
Return to oven till heated through, about 10
minutes. Serves 6.

Braised Courgettes

50 calories per serving

4 large courgettes
½ oz (12 gm) butter
½ teaspoon salt
Dash of coarsely ground pepper
1 medium onion, thinly sliced and
  separated into rings
1 medium tomato, cut into wedges
2 oz (50 gm) mushrooms, sliced

Wash courgettes well, remove ends and cut into
slices. Melt butter in a large frying pan and add
salt and pepper. Cook onion in butter till crisp-
tender, then add courgette slices. Cook, covered,
for 6 minutes, stirring occasionally. Add tomato
and mushrooms. Continue cooking, covered, till
tomato and mushrooms are hot and courgettes
are crisp-tender, about 4 minutes. Remove vegetables to a serving dish with a slotted spoon.
Serves 6.

Onion and Potato Bake

87 calories per serving

2 medium potatoes, peeled and thinly
  sliced
3 medium onions, thinly sliced
Salt and pepper
¼ pint (125 ml) skimmed milk
2 tablespoons chopped pimiento
2 tablespoons chopped parsley
2 oz (50 gm) processed cheese, grated

Layer half the potatoes and half the onions in a
greased baking dish, 1¾ inches deep and about 10
by 6 inches. Sprinkle generously with salt and
pepper. Combine milk, pimiento and parsley, and
pour half the mixture over the onion-potato layer.
Repeat layers. Cover, and bake at Gas No 4 or
350°F (177°C) till vegetables are tender, about
1 hour. Uncover. Sprinkle cheese over top, and
return to oven till it melts. Serves 6.

Onion, Potato and Mushroom Bake

Make exactly as above, using 2 tablespoons very
finely chopped mushrooms instead of the pimiento.

LOW-CALORIE

COOKING TIP

*Keep vegetable dishes
low in calories*

Substitute lemon juice or herbs for butter or
margarine to add flavour to vegetables and to
keep the calorie count to a minimum. For example,
boil sliced carrots and cubed turnips till tender,
about 15 minutes, then toss them in chopped
parsley and 1 teaspoon lemon juice, to make a
tasty vegetable dish.

Baked Devilled Tomatoes

51 calories per serving

4 large tomatoes, halved
Salt
1 tablespoon prepared mustard
2 tablespoons chopped green pepper
2 tablespoons chopped celery
1 tablespoon chopped green onion
1½ oz (37 gm) butter or margarine, melted

Place tomatoes, cut side up, in a baking dish. Sprinkle with salt. Spread cut side of tomatoes with mustard. Combine rest of ingredients; spoon mixture over tomatoes. Bake at Gas No 7 or 425°F (218°C) for 8 to 10 minutes. Serves 8.

Vegetable Fiesta

62 calories per serving

8 medium tomatoes, skinned
1 can (12 oz or 300 gm) whole kernel corn
1 medium green pepper, coarsely chopped
¼ teaspoon celery seed
Dash of ground oregano
1½ teaspoons salt
Dash of pepper

Cut tomatoes into wedges. Put into a saucepan with all remaining ingredients. Cook, uncovered, over medium heat till green pepper is tender, 8 to 10 minutes. Stir occasionally. Serves 6.

Cabbage Scramble

45 calories per serving

½ pint (250 ml) water
2 teaspoons yeast extract
¼ teaspoon oregano
½ small head cabbage, shredded
3 medium carrots, shredded
1 medium onion, thinly sliced

In an 8 inch frying pan, combine water, yeast extract and oregano. Add all vegetables to mixture in pan. Cook, covered, over low heat, till vegetables are tender, about 15 to 20 minutes, and stir occasionally. Drain before serving. Serves 4.

Creamy Brussels Sprouts

62 calories per serving

1 lb (½ kilo) Brussels sprouts
1 can (5 oz or 125 gm) water chestnuts, drained and sliced
1 packet (3 oz or 75 gm) cream cheese
3 tablespoons skimmed milk
½ teaspoon prepared mustard
1 teaspoon lemon juice
Dash of salt

Cook sprouts until tender. Do not drain. Add water chestnuts and heat through. Blend cream cheese with skimmed milk, add mustard, lemon juice and salt, and beat well. Stir over low heat until hot. Drain sprouts and chestnuts, and pour cheese sauce over. Serves 8.

Corn Medley

50 calories per serving

1 packet (10 oz or 250 gm) frozen whole kernel corn
2 medium celery stalks, chopped
1 chicken stock cube, crumbled
4 tablespoons water
2 oz (50 gm) mushrooms, sliced
1 medium tomato, cut into thin wedges
Salt and pepper

In a saucepan combine corn, celery, stock cube and water. Bring to boil, cover and simmer till vegetables are tender, about 5 to 7 minutes. Stir in mushrooms and tomato wedges, and heat through. Season to taste. Serves 6.

Mix courgettes with tomato wedges, onion rings and sliced mushrooms for a colourful vegetable dish.

Almond Butter Cauliflower

52 calories per serving

1 large cauliflower
1 oz (25 gm) butter
1 oz (25 gm) fresh white breadcrumbs
6 blanched almonds, chopped
¼ level teaspoon rosemary
Paprika

Break cauliflower into florets and cook in boiling salted water till crisp-tender. Meanwhile, heat butter in a frying pan, add breadcrumbs and almonds and fry slowly until golden, turning frequently. Drain cauliflower and put into serving bowl. Coat with crumb mixture and sprinkle with rosemary and paprika. Serves 6.

Creamed Parsnips

85 calories per serving

1 lb (½ kilo) parsnips
½ oz (12 gm) instant low-fat milk granules
1–2 teaspoons curry powder
½ teaspoon paprika
Large pinch of ground nutmeg
1 tablespoon chopped parsley

Peel and slice parsnips. Cook in boiling salted water until very tender. Drain, stand pan over low heat and mash finely. Add rest of ingredients. Beat until hot and fluffy. Serves 6.

Bean Casserole

54 calories per serving

1 lb (½ kilo) green beans, sliced
2 green peppers, cut into strips
2 onions, thinly sliced
2 oz (50 gm) lean ham, chopped
Salt and pepper
3 tablespoons water

Fill a casserole dish with alternate layers of beans, peppers, onions and ham. Sprinkle salt and pepper between layers and pour water into dish. Cover tightly and cook at Gas No 4 or 350°F (177°C) for 1¼ hours. Serves 6.

Sauerkraut Hot-pot

58 calories per serving

4 breakfast cups undrained sauerkraut
1 large cooking apple, grated
4 tablespoons dry white wine
2 cloves
1–2 drops of liquid sugar substitute

Put undrained sauerkraut into a saucepan with rest of ingredients. Cover and simmer gently for 20 to 30 minutes, stirring frequently. Serves 4.

Stewed Tomatoes

63 calories per serving

½ oz (12 gm) butter
2 medium celery stalks, chopped
1 small onion, chopped
1 lb (½ kilo) tomatoes, skinned and chopped
½ teaspoon basil
1 teaspoon salt
Freshly milled pepper
1 tablespoon chopped parsley

Heat butter in pan and add celery and onion. Cover and cook gently for 10 minutes or until crisp-tender. Add all remaining ingredients, then cover and simmer for 15 minutes. Serves 4.

Baked Cabbage

81 calories per serving

1 small head white cabbage, shredded
Salt and pepper
½ pint (250 ml) skimmed milk
1 teaspoon paprika
½ oz (12 gm) breadcrumbs, lightly toasted
1 oz (25 gm) Cheddar cheese, grated

Put cabbage into a large casserole dish and sprinkle liberally with salt and pepper. Pour milk into the dish, and sprinkle with paprika and crumbs. Cover and bake at Gas No 3 or 325°F (163°C) for 45 minutes. Uncover, sprinkle with cheese and brown quickly under grill. Serves 4.

Dressed Celeriac

36 calories per serving

2 medium celeriac
1 medium onion, sliced
¼ pint (125 ml) low-calorie dressing
  (page 8)
3 anchovy fillets, chopped
2 heaped tablespoons chopped parsley

Peel celeriac fairly thickly, and slice. Cook celeriac and onion in boiling salted water until tender. Drain, and return to saucepan. Add dressing, anchovies and parsley. Toss over medium heat until hot. Serves 4.

Artichokes in Sauce

74 calories per serving

12 small Jerusalem artichokes
1–2 teaspoons lemon juice
1 oz (25 gm) butter
1 tablespoon flour
½ pint (250 ml) skimmed milk
Salt and pepper
Dash of nutmeg
Paprika

Peel artichokes, and drop into a saucepan of boiling salted water containing the lemon juice. Cook for about 15 minutes or until tender. Meanwhile, heat butter in a saucepan. Stir in flour and cook for 2 minutes without browning. Gradually blend in skimmed milk. Cook, stirring, until sauce is thick and bubbly. Add salt, pepper and nutmeg to taste. Drain artichokes and put into serving bowl. Coat with sauce and dust with paprika. Serves 6.

Cheesy Chicory

69 calories per serving

6 heads of chicory
2 teaspoons lemon juice
1 tablespoon cornflour
½ pint (250 ml) skimmed milk
Salt and pepper
Dash of ground nutmeg
2 oz (50 gm) Cheddar cheese, grated
Paprika

Remove discoloured leaves from chicory, and discard. Cook in boiling salted water, to which lemon juice has been added, until crisp-tender, about 10 to 15 minutes. Meanwhile, blend cornflour smoothly with half the milk. Put into saucepan, add rest of milk, salt and pepper to taste, and nutmeg. Cook, stirring, till thickened and bubbly. Add half the cheese and stir till melted. Drain chicory, put into a serving dish and coat with sauce. Sprinkle rest of cheese on top, add dusting of paprika and brown under a hot grill. Serves 6.

Bacon Beans

58 calories per serving

1 lb (½ kilo) runner beans, sliced
½ oz (12 gm) butter
2 rashers streaky bacon, chopped
Large pinch of marjoram

Cook beans in boiling salted water until crisp-tender. Drain and return to saucepan with butter. Fry bacon till crisp, and add to beans with marjoram. Heat through. Serves 4.

Almonds and rosemary impart a special flavour to Almond Butter Cauliflower.

Salads
for the Calorie Counter

Chicken-artichoke Bowl

245 calories per serving

- ¼ pint (125 ml)+1½ tablespoons low-calorie dressing (page 8)
- 2 tablespoons water
- 4 thin slices onion, separated into rings
- 1 clove garlic, finely chopped
- ¼ teaspoon celery salt
- ½ teaspoon salt
- Dash of pepper
- 6 canned artichoke hearts
- 2 tablespoons chopped canned pimiento
- 3 large chicken breasts, skinned, boned and cooked
- 1 large Webb lettuce, shredded

In a medium saucepan combine salad dressing, water, onion, garlic, celery salt, and salt and pepper. Bring to boil and add artichoke hearts. Cook hearts for about 3 minutes, stir in chopped pimiento and chill. Cut chicken into cubes.

At serving time, drain chilled artichoke mixture, reserving marinade. Cut artichokes into bite-sized pieces. Combine artichoke mixture with chicken cubes, lettuce and enough of the reserved marinade to coat, then toss lightly. Serves 6.

Chicken, Corn and Cabbage Salad

180 calories per serving

- 1 can (12 oz or 300 gm) whole kernel corn
- 8 oz (200 gm) cooked diced chicken
- ½ small head of white cabbage, shredded
- 1 medium green pepper, de-seeded and chopped
- ¼ pint (125 ml) low-calorie dressing (page 8)
- 2 tomatoes, skinned and cut into wedges

Put corn, chicken, cabbage and green pepper into a bowl. Add dressing and toss thoroughly. Garnish with wedges of tomato. Serves 4.

Chicken and Lettuce Salad

121 calories per serving

- 1 cos lettuce, torn into bite-size pieces
- 8 oz (200 gm) cooked diced chicken
- 2 tablespoons grated Parmesan cheese
- ¼ pint (125 ml) low-calorie dressing (page 8)
- 4 teaspoons tarragon vinegar
- ½ teaspoon dry mustard
- ¼ teaspoon Worcestershire sauce
- 2 slices of toast, diced

Combine lettuce, chicken and Parmesan. Mix dressing and next three ingredients. Toss half the mixture with diced toast, but do not soak. Add to salad with remaining dressing. Serves 6.

Peach and Chicken Cups

220 calories per serving

- 2 medium chicken breasts, skinned, boned and cooked
- 3 oz (75 gm) curd cheese
- 3 tablespoons low-calorie dressing (page 8)
- ¼ teaspoon thyme
- ⅛ teaspoon basil
- Salt and pepper
- 1 can (1 lb or ½ kilo) peach halves, drained and diced
- 1 medium celery stalk, chopped
- 1 green pepper, sliced into thick rings
- Lettuce leaves

Cube chicken. Mix cheese, next three ingredients, and a dash of salt and pepper. Add chicken, peaches and celery, and toss. Chill. Spoon mixture into the pepper rings and serve on lettuce. Serves 4.

Decorate Chicken and Lettuce Salad with a tomato rose. The chicken, Parmesan and croûtons make an original mixture, and cos lettuce gives a crunchy texture.

Super Chef Salad

154 calories per serving

1 large lettuce, shredded
2 tomatoes, cut into wedges
3 hard-boiled eggs, quartered
1 small onion, sliced and separated into rings
4 oz (100 gm) ham, cut into thin strips
4 oz (100 gm) Cheddar cheese, cut into strips
6 tablespoons low-calorie dressing (page 8)

In a large salad bowl arrange lettuce, tomatoes, eggs, onion, ham and cheese. Add dressing and toss. Serves 8.

Ham and Cheese Medley

246 calories per serving

1 small can pineapple titbits, drained
4 oz (100 gm) ham, cubed
4 oz (100 gm) grapes, halved and de-seeded
2 oz (50 gm) Mozzarella cheese, cut into strips
8 oz (200 gm) cottage cheese
6 tablespoons skimmed milk
½ teaspoon paprika
1 medium lettuce, shredded

Combine first four ingredients in a large bowl and chill. In a blender goblet combine cottage cheese, skimmed milk and paprika, and blend till smooth. Add lettuce to ham mixture and toss. Transfer to four individual bowls and accompany with cheese dressing. Serves 4.

Cottage Cheese and Prawn Salad

165 calories per serving

1 large lettuce, shredded
Salt and pepper
1 tablespoon salad oil
1 tablespoon wine vinegar
12 oz (300 gm) peeled prawns
12 oz (300 gm) cottage cheese
1 small pickled cucumber, chopped
2 tablespoons sliced onion

In a bowl sprinkle lettuce with salt and pepper, then toss with oil and vinegar. Reserve a few whole prawns and coarsely chop remainder. Toss prawns and remaining ingredients with lettuce. Garnish with whole prawns. Serves 6.

Curried Prawn Salad

119 calories per serving

Use tinned or frozen prawns for convenience

8 oz (200 gm) prawns
2 tablespoons lemon juice
3 medium celery stalks, thinly sliced
2 tablespoons chopped parsley
½ teaspoon curry powder
6 tablespoons low-calorie dressing (page 8)
1 medium lettuce, shredded
3 hard-boiled eggs, sliced
Salt and pepper

Sprinkle prawns with lemon juice, and add celery and parsley. Stir curry powder into dressing and add to prawn mixture. Chill, then just before serving toss mixture with lettuce and hard-boiled eggs. Season to taste with salt and pepper. Serves 6.

Scallop Toss

178 calories per serving

Serve with melba toast for a special lunch

12 oz (300 gm) scallops
1 clove garlic
1 medium lettuce, shredded
12 oz (300 gm) spinach, shredded
3 hard-boiled eggs, quartered
2 medium celery stalks, sliced
4 oz (100 gm) Mozzarella cheese, cut into thin strips
4 tablespoons low-calorie dressing (page 8)

Cook scallops in boiling salted water for 5 minutes. Drain and chill. Rub a salad bowl with cut garlic clove. Put lettuce, spinach, eggs, celery, cheese and scallops into bowl. Add dressing and toss. Serves 6.

LOW-CALORIE

COOKING TIP

Make tomato cups to hold salad mixtures. Cut tops off tomatoes and scoop out pulp with a spoon. Turn tomatoes, cut side down, on absorbent paper towelling to drain before stuffing. Chop pulp and use in salad.

Tuna-fruit Salad

160 calories per serving

- 2 medium apples, unpeeled and cut into ½ inch cubes
- 1 medium lettuce, shredded
- 1 can (7½ oz or 185 gm) tuna, drained and flaked
- 1 breakfast cup seedless grapes
- 4 tablespoons mayonnaise
- ¼ pint (125 ml) low-calorie dressing (page 8)

Toss together apples, lettuce, tuna, and grapes. Cover and chill. Combine mayonnaise with dressing, and toss with tuna mixture. Serves 6.

Dieter's Tuna Salad

78 calories per serving

- ¼ pint (125 ml)+1½ tablespoons wine vinegar
- 2 teaspoons sugar
- 1½ teaspoons dried basil
- Dash of pepper
- 1 large crisp lettuce, shredded
- 2 cans (each 7½ oz or 185 gm) tuna, drained and flaked
- 8 small tomatoes, skinned and halved
- ½ medium onion, thinly sliced and separated into rings
- 1 medium cucumber, sliced
- 1 medium celery stalk, chopped

Mix first four ingredients and chill. Toss lettuce with remaining ingredients. Add dressing and toss lightly. Serves 8.

Prawn-stuffed Tomatoes

107 calories per serving

- 6 large tomatoes
- 1 teaspoon garlic salt
- 1 small onion, chopped
- 1 medium celery stalk, chopped
- 2 tablespoons chopped green pepper
- Dash of pepper
- 8 oz (200 gm) peeled prawns, chopped
- 1 small slice of toast, cut into small dice
- Parsley (optional)

Cut tops off tomatoes and scoop out pulp. Chop tops and pulp and drain well. Sprinkle inside of tomatoes with garlic salt. In a medium frying pan, combine tomato pulp, onion, celery, green pepper and pepper. Simmer, covered, till vegetables are tender, about 10 to 15 minutes. Stir in prawns and toast dice. Pile mixture into tomato shells. Place in a baking dish, 1¾ inches deep and about 10 by 6 inches, then pour water into dish ½ inch deep. Bake at Gas No 5 or 375°F (191°C) for 20 to 25 minutes. Garnish with parsley, if liked. Serves 6.

Chicken-stuffed Tomatoes

124 calories per serving

Make exactly as Prawn-stuffed Tomatoes, but use 8 oz (200 gm) finely chopped cooked white chicken instead of the prawns. Serves 6.

Crab-artichoke Toss

122 calories per serving

- 1 medium can artichoke hearts
- 1 medium cos or Webb lettuce, shredded
- 1 tomato, cut into wedges
- 1 can (7½ oz or 185 gm) crab meat, drained and broken into pieces
- 2 oz (50 gm) processed cheese, cut into strips
- 1 large carrot, grated
- 1 medium onion, thinly sliced
- 5 tablespoons low-calorie dressing (page 8)

Drain artichoke hearts on soft kitchen paper and cut each in half. Toss with remaining ingredients. Serves 6.

Combine calorie counting with entertaining and serve Crab-tomato Aspic bursting with crab meat and crisp celery.

Crab-tomato Aspic

125 calories per serving

A tasty and original aspic dish

  2 envelopes (about 6 teaspoons) gelatine
  ½ pint (250 ml) cold beef stock
  1¼ pints (¾ litre) tomato juice
  2 slices of onion
  2 bay leaves
  ¼ teaspoon celery salt
  2 tablespoons lemon juice
  3 medium celery stalks, chopped
  1 can (7½ oz or 185 gm) crab meat,
    drained and flaked
  3 hard-boiled eggs, cut into wedges

Soften gelatine in ¼ pint (125 ml) cold beef stock. Combine tomato juice, onion, bay leaves and celery salt, and bring to boil. Remove onion and bay leaves. Add softened gelatine, and stir till dissolved. Add an additional ¼ pint (125 ml) beef stock and the lemon juice. Chill till partially set. Fold in celery and crab meat, and turn into a 2½ pint (1½ litre) mould. Chill till firm. Unmould and garnish with hard-boiled eggs. Serves 6.

Blender Cucumber Salad

88 calories per serving

  1 large cucumber
  1 envelope (about 3 teaspoons) gelatine
  2 tablespoons sugar
  ¼ pint (125 ml)+5 tablespoons
    unsweetened pineapple juice
  4 teaspoons lemon juice
  1–2 drops of yellow food colouring

  YOGURT DRESSING:
  3 tablespoons natural yogurt
  1½ tablespoons low-calorie dressing
    (page 8)
  1½ teaspoons sugar
  ½ teaspoon lemon juice

Peel cucumber, halve lengthwise and remove seeds. Slice into blender container, cover and blend on high speed till puréed. Stop blender, as needed, to push cucumber down from sides of container. Add water to purée, if necessary, to make ½ pint (250 ml). In a medium saucepan combine gelatine and sugar, and add pineapple juice and food colouring. Chill till partially sugar are dissolved. Add puréed cucumber, lemon juice and food colouring. Chill till partially thickened, stirring occasionally. Pour the cucumber mixture into a 1½ pint (¾ litre) mould, and chill till firm. Serves 4.

Serve with **Yogurt Dressing**: combine all ingredients and chill.

Tangy Seafood Toss

212 calories per serving

  1 tablespoon cornflour
  1 tablespoon sugar
  ½ teaspoon paprika
  ½ teaspoon dry mustard
  ¼ teaspoon salt
  ⅛ teaspoon pepper
  1 can (1 lb or ½ kilo) grapefruit segments
  3 tablespoons tomato ketchup
  2 tablespoons salad oil
  1 medium lettuce, shredded
  1 can (7½ oz or 185 gm) tuna, drained and
    broken into chunks
  ½ small cucumber, sliced
  6 radishes, sliced

Mix cornflour and next five ingredients. Drain grapefruit segments, reserving liquid. Blend reserved liquid into cornflour mixture. Cook, stirring, till thick and bubbly. Remove from heat, and stir in tomato ketchup and salad oil. Chill. In a bowl, arrange rest of ingredients and the grapefruit segments. Chill, and serve with the cooked dressing. Serves 4.

Salmon-stuffed Tomatoes

191 calories per serving

1 large can (1 lb or ½ kilo) pink salmon,
  drained
8 oz (200 gm) cottage cheese
3 tablespoons low-calorie dressing
  (page 8)
1 medium celery stalk, chopped
2 tablespoons chopped green pepper
¼ teaspoon onion salt
Dash of pepper
6 medium tomatoes, chilled
Lettuce
6 lemon wedges

In a medium-sized bowl flake salmon, removing bones and skin. Add cottage cheese, dressing, celery, green pepper, onion salt and pepper. Mix well, then chill. With stem end down, cut each tomato into six wedges, cutting to, but not through the base of the tomato. Spread wedges apart slightly and sprinkle lightly with salt. Spoon equal amounts of salmon mixture into each tomato. Serve stuffed tomatoes on lettuce-lined plates. Garnish with lemon wedges. Serves 6.

Sunshine Aspic

65 calories per serving

½ pint (250 ml)+3 tablespoons tomato
  juice
1 bay leaf
¼ teaspoon celery salt
¼ teaspoon onion salt
1 envelope (about 3 teaspoons) gelatine
¼ pint (125 ml) water
2 tablespoons lemon juice
2 hard-boiled eggs, sliced

Combine half the tomato juice with bay leaf, celery salt and onion salt, then simmer, uncovered, for 5 minutes. Remove and discard bay leaf. Meanwhile, soften gelatine in remaining cold tomato juice, add to hot juice mixture and stir to dissolve gelatine. Stir in water and lemon juice. Chill till mixture is partially set. Pour half the chilled mixture into a 1½ pint (¾ litre) ring mould. Press egg slices gently into gelatine along outer edge of the mould. Carefully pour remaining gelatine around and over egg slices. Chill till firm, then unmould. Serves 4.

Orange Perfection Salad

48 calories per serving

1 envelope (about 3 teaspoons) gelatine
2 tablespoons sugar
¼ teaspoon salt
¼ pint (125 ml)+5 tablespoons cold water
¼ pint (125 ml) orange juice
1 tablespoon lemon juice
1 tablespoon vinegar
2 drops of yellow food colouring
1 medium orange, sectioned and diced
1 breakfast cup cabbage, shredded
3 medium celery stalks, finely chopped

In a medium saucepan mix gelatine, sugar and salt; add 5 tablespoons cold water. Stir over low heat till gelatine and sugar are dissolved. Stir in ¼ pint (125 ml) water, orange juice, lemon juice, vinegar and food colouring. Chill till partially set. Fold in remaining ingredients, and turn into a 1½ pint (¾ litre) mould. Chill till firm. Serves 6.

The refreshing goodness of oranges, shredded cabbage and chopped celery go to make up this glistening Orange Perfection Salad.

Perfect for a summer lunch is this Raspberry-cheese
Mould with cottage cheese and celery filling.

LOW-CALORIE

COOKING TIP

*Keep calories
low in salad
dressings*

Retain low calorie count of salads—toss crisp,
green salads with lemon juice, vinegar, or cream-
style cottage cheese before serving.

Carrot and Orange Salad

59 calories per serving

1 lb (½ kilo) carrots, cut into ½ inch slices
1 orange
6 tablespoons low-calorie dressing
  (page 8)
2 tablespoons sliced onion
1 tablespoon chopped parsley
½ teaspoon grated orange peel
¼ teaspoon salt
Lettuce leaves

Cook carrots in boiling water till crisp-tender,
about 8 to 10 minutes, and drain. Slice three thin
slices from end of unpeeled orange. Halve slices
and add to carrots. Squeeze rest of orange to make
3 tablespoons juice. Combine dressing, orange
juice, onion, parsley, orange peel and salt, then
stir into carrots. Cover and chill. Serve in lettuce
cups with dressing. Serves 6.

Raspberry-cheese Mould

101 calories per serving

½ pint (250 ml)+4 tablespoons water
1 packet (10 oz or 250 gm) frozen
  raspberries
2 packets raspberry-flavoured jelly
1 teaspoon gelatine
12 oz (300 gm) cottage cheese
2 celery stalks, chopped

Add ½ pint (250 ml) water to frozen raspberries,
and bring to boil. Add jellies and stir until melted.
Make up to 2 pints (1¼ litres) with cold water.
Pour half the mixture into a 3 pint (1¾ litre) ring
mould (leave remainder at room temperature) and
chill till mixture in mould is almost firm. Soften
gelatine in 4 tablespoons cold water and heat till
dissolved. Stir into cottage cheese with celery, and
mix well. Pour into mould, chill till almost firm,
then pour reserved raspberry mixture over cheese
layer. Chill till firm. Serves 8.

Dill Tomato Slices

33 calories per serving

4 tablespoons low-calorie dressing
  (page 8)
3 tablespoons water
½ teaspoon dried dill
½ teaspoon salt
⅛ teaspoon pepper
1 large cucumber, unpeeled
3 medium tomatoes, sliced
Lettuce leaves

Combine salad dressing, water, dill, salt and
pepper. Using a vegetable parer, slice cucumber
paper-thin into a shallow dish. Add marinade, and
cover and chill for 6 hours or overnight.

   To serve, arrange tomato slices on top of
lettuce leaves on a serving platter or individual
plates. Spoon on marinated cucumber and marinade. Serves 6.

Sunshine Apple Mould

80 calories per serving

1 small can crushed pineapple
Apple juice
1 envelope (about 3 teaspoons) gelatine
Few drops of yellow food colouring
2 eating apples, peeled, cored and diced
Lettuce leaves

Thoroughly drain pineapple, and make up juice from can to ¾ pint (375 ml) with apple juice. Pour into saucepan, add gelatine, and stir over low heat until gelatine dissolves. Stir in food colouring. Chill till partially set, then fold in drained pineapple together with apples. Transfer to a 1½ pint (¾ litre) mould. Chill until firm. To serve, unmould the salad on a lettuce-lined plate. Serves 6.

Sauerkraut Salad

39 calories per serving

1 lb (½ kilo) sauerkraut, drained
3 medium carrots, grated
1 small green pepper, de-seeded and
  chopped
1 small onion, finely chopped
3 tablespoons low-calorie dressing
  (page 8)
½ teaspoon poppy seeds
Lettuce leaves

Combine sauerkraut, carrots, pepper and onion. Mix dressing with poppy seeds, add to vegetables and toss. Chill thoroughly, then serve on lettuce leaves. Serves 6.

Artichoke-fruit Salad

62 calories per serving

1 medium can artichoke hearts, drained
3 tablespoons low-calorie dressing
  (page 8)
2 tablespoons vinegar
1 teaspoon Worcestershire sauce
1 tablespoon chopped parsley
½ teaspoon salt
Dash of pepper
1 large Webb or cos lettuce, shredded
½ a curly endive, shredded
2 grapefruit, peeled and sectioned

Halve artichokes. Combine dressing and next five ingredients. Mix well. Pour over artichokes, then chill, covered, for 3 to 4 hours or overnight. In a large bowl combine remaining ingredients. Add artichokes with dressing and toss. Serves 8.

Pineapple Mould Salad

55 calories per serving

1 medium can crushed pineapple
Low-calorie bitter lemon
1 envelope (about 3 teaspoons) gelatine
1 dessertspoon lemon juice
Few drops of green food colouring
1 small grapefruit, cut into segments
2 tablespoons grated cucumber, well
  drained

Drain pineapple, reserving juice. Make up to ¾ pint (375 ml) with bitter lemon. Soften gelatine in half the mixture, and stir over low heat until gelatine dissolves. Stir in remaining juice mixture, lemon juice and food colouring; chill till partially set. Fold in remaining ingredients, and pour into a 2 pint (1¼ litre) mould. Chill till firm. Serves 4.

Toss crisp greens and grapefruit sections with marinated artichoke hearts to make an Artichoke-fruit Salad.

Broccoli Salad Bowl

95 calories per serving

1 lb (½ kilo) broccoli
9 tablespoons low-calorie dressing
  (page 8)
1 small dill pickle, finely chopped
1 small green pepper, finely chopped
2 tablespoons chopped parsley
1 tablespoon drained capers
2 hard-boiled eggs, chopped
Lettuce leaves

Trim ends of broccoli and peel stems if tough. Cook in 1 inch salted water till crisp-tender, about 10 to 12 minutes; drain thoroughly. Combine dressing, dill pickle, green pepper, parsley, and capers. Stir in chopped eggs. Spoon dressing mixture over broccoli spears, then cover and chill for several hours or overnight. Arrange broccoli on lettuce leaves. Serves 6.

Herbed Bean Salad

50 calories per serving

1 packet (9 oz or 225 gm) frozen cut
  green beans
3 large celery stalks, sliced
1 onion, sliced and separated into rings
4 tablespoons low-calorie dressing
  (page 8)
1 tablespoon finely chopped canned
  pimiento
¼–½ teaspoon oregano
Dash of salt
Lettuce leaves

Cook beans according to packet directions and drain. Mix beans, celery and onion. Blend together dressing, pimiento, oregano and salt. Toss with vegetable mixture. Chill for several hours or overnight, stirring occasionally. Serve in lettuce cups. Serves 5.

Bean and Carrot Salad

83 calories per serving

- 1 breakfast cup canned cut green beans
- 1 breakfast cup canned sliced carrots
- 1 breakfast cup canned red kidney beans
- 1 small onion, thinly sliced
- 2 tablespoons chopped celery
- 2 tablespoons chopped green pepper
- 1 tablespoon chopped parsley
- 9 tablespoons low-calorie dressing (page 8)

Arrange canned vegetables, onion and celery in a shallow dish. Sprinkle with green pepper and parsley. Pour dressing over vegetable mixture, cover and refrigerate for several hours or overnight. Toss vegetables before serving. Serves 6.

Serve robust Bean and Carrot Salad with grilled meat. Arrange vegetables in a chilled salad bowl and add a salad dressing marinade.

Asparagus Vinaigrette

74 calories per serving

- 1 medium can (10 oz or 250 gm) asparagus spears, drained
- 6 tablespoons low-calorie dressing (page 8)
- 2 tablespoons dry white wine
- 2 tablespoons finely sliced onion
- 2 tablespoons finely chopped green pepper
- 1 tablespoon finely chopped parsley
- 1 tablespoon drained and chopped pickled cucumber
- Lettuce leaves
- 2 small tomatoes, chilled and sliced

Arrange drained asparagus spears in a shallow dish. Combine dressing, white wine, onion, green pepper, parsley and pickled cucumber; mix well. Top asparagus spears with dressing; cover and chill for several hours or overnight, spooning over spears occasionally.

To serve, drain spears, reserving dressing. For each salad, arrange a few spears on top of a lettuce leaf, and top with a few tomato slices. Spoon a little reserved dressing over each salad. Serves 4.

44

Parmesan Tomatoes

50 calories per serving

6 large tomatoes, skinned and sliced
¼ pint (125 ml) low-calorie dressing
    (page 8)
1 clove garlic, very finely chopped
Salt and freshly milled pepper
4 tablespoons grated Parmesan cheese
1 tablespoon finely chopped parsley

Arrange three sliced tomatoes, in a single layer, on a flat plate. Sprinkle with half the dressing, half the garlic, salt and pepper, and half the cheese. Add rest of tomato slices, and sprinkle with remaining ingredients. Cover and chill. Serves 4.

Tomato, Grapefruit and Anchovy Salad

90 calories per serving

6 large tomatoes, skinned
2 medium grapefruit
1 can anchovies in oil
12 stuffed olives
2 teaspoons grated onion
6 tablespoons low-calorie dressing
    (page 8)

Slice tomatoes. Peel grapefruit and divide the flesh into segments by cutting in between membranes. Arrange tomatoes and grapefruit segments in rows on a flat plate. Garnish with a criss-cross of anchovies and whole olives. Sprinkle with onion and dressing. Serves 6.

Green Bean and Mushroom Salad

45 calories per serving

8 oz (200 gm) cooked sliced beans
4 oz (100 gm) raw mushrooms, sliced
1 hard-boiled egg, chopped
2 medium celery stalks, thinly sliced
1 canned pimiento, finely chopped
6 tablespoons low-calorie dressing
    (page 8)

Put beans into a bowl, add all remaining ingredients and toss thoroughly. Serves 4.

Cabbage, Carrot and Raisin Slaw

54 calories per serving

1 medium head of white cabbage
2 large carrots, grated
1 oz (25 gm) seedless raisins
1 small green pepper, de-seeded and
    chopped
1 medium onion, grated
1 teaspoon finely grated lemon peel
6 tablespoons low-calorie dressing
    (page 8)

Finely shred cabbage, and put into a bowl. Add all remaining ingredients and toss. Serves 6.

Orange and Pear Seafood Salad

65 calories per serving

4 medium oranges
2 ripe dessert pears
4 oz (100 gm) peeled prawns
1 tablespoon finely chopped chives
4 tablespoons low-calorie dressing
    (page 8)

Peel oranges and slice thinly. Peel pears and cut each lengthwise into six segments; remove cores. Stand orange slices on a flat plate, and arrange pear segments on top. Sprinkle with prawns, chives and dressing. Serves 4.

Tomato, Grapefruit and Anchovy Salad is one exciting salad idea for the reluctant dieter.

Brussels Sprout and Water Chestnut Salad

86 calories per serving

  1 lb (½ kilo) baby Brussels sprouts
  12 canned water chestnuts, sliced
  2 canned pineapple rings, chopped
  1 green pepper, de-seeded and chopped
  ¼ pint (125 ml) natural yogurt
  1–2 teaspoons curry powder
  1 tablespoon Soy sauce
  ½ teaspoon garlic salt
  1 tablespoon lemon juice
  Liquid artificial sweetener to taste
  1 teaspoon paprika

Cook sprouts in boiling salted water until crisp-tender, then drain. Leave until cold and put into a bowl. Add chestnuts, pineapple and pepper. Beat yogurt with all remaining ingredients and half the paprika. Add to salad and toss. Sprinkle with rest of the paprika. Serves 4.

Cauliflower Caper Salad

154 calories per serving

  1 large cauliflower
  1 tablespoon chopped capers
  1 small avocado, peeled and diced
  4 tomatoes, skinned and cut into wedges
  2 oz (50 gm) Danish blue cheese, crumbled
  6 tablespoons low-calorie dressing (page 8)

Cook cauliflower in boiling salted water until crisp-tender. Drain, divide head into florets and put into a bowl. Add all remaining ingredients and toss. Serves 6.

Cucumber Yogurt Salad

33 calories per serving

  1 clove garlic
  1 large cucumber
  1 medium mild onion, thinly sliced
  2 teaspoons finely chopped fresh mint
  ¼ pint (125 ml) natural yogurt
  Salt and freshly milled pepper to taste

Cut garlic clove in half and rub round inside of a salad bowl. Wash and dry cucumber, cut into very thin slices and put into bowl. Add onion and mint. Beat yogurt with salt and pepper to taste. Add to salad and toss. Serves 4.

Apple and Cabbage Slaw

64 calories per serving

  1 medium head (1½ lb or ¾ kilo) of white cabbage
  4 rosy apples
  Lemon juice
  1 small green pepper, de-seeded and chopped
  1 medium onion, thinly sliced
  6 tablespoons low-calorie dressing (page 8)
  1 oz (25 gm) Edam cheese, grated

Shred cabbage finely, and put into a bowl. Wash and dry apples, remove centre cores and cut into slices. Sprinkle with lemon juice to prevent browning, then add to bowl. Add green pepper and onion to bowl with dressing, and toss. Sprinkle with cheese. Serves 6.

Aubergine Salad

81 calories per serving

  1 large aubergine
  1 medium onion, chopped
  1 clove garlic, chopped
  2 large tomatoes, skinned and cut into wedges
  3 tablespoons low-calorie dressing (page 8)
  2 tablespoons natural yogurt
  12 thin slices of cucumber
  2 hard-boiled eggs, cut into wedges

Wash aubergine and wipe dry. Stand on a baking tray without peeling. Bake in the centre of a moderately hot oven at Gas No 5 or 375°F (190°C) for 45 minutes, or until tender when pierced with a cocktail stick or fork. Peel when cool enough to handle, then wrap and chill in the refrigerator. Later, cut aubergine into small cubes, and put into a bowl. Add onion, garlic and tomatoes. Beat dressing and yogurt well together, pour over salad, and toss. Garnish with cucumber and egg. Serves 4.

Slenderizing Sandwiches

Fruit Wheels

140 calories per serving

2 bagles (Jewish ring rolls)
1 tablespoon cream cheese, softened
Ground cinnamon
1 fresh medium peach
½ medium banana
Lemon juice
4 thin slices of honeydew melon

Split and toast bagles, spread with cream cheese and sprinkle with cinnamon. Thinly slice peach and banana, then dip slices in lemon juice to prevent darkening. To serve, arrange sliced fruit with slices of honeydew melon on top of bagles. Makes 4.

Open Chicken Sandwiches

139 calories per serving

2 tablespoons flour
1 tablespoon sugar
1 teaspoon dry mustard
½ teaspoon salt
Dash of cayenne
2 egg yolks, lightly beaten
¼ pint (125 ml)+1 tablespoon skimmed milk
3 tablespoons vinegar
1 small can water chestnuts, drained and sliced
Paprika
8 slices of whole wheat bread
Watercress
8 slices of cooked chicken

Mix flour, sugar, mustard, salt and cayenne, then stir in egg yolks and skimmed milk. Cook, stirring, over very low heat till thick and bubbly. Stir in vinegar and chill. Roll edges of a few water chestnuts in paprika, then set aside. Spread bread with some of the dressing, and top each slice with some watercress, a slice of chicken, and a few water chestnuts. Top with slices of paprika-edged water chestnuts. Pass remaining dressing. Makes 8.

Ham and Salad Rolls

207 calories per serving

4 bap rolls, split
4 teaspoons prepared mustard
½ small lettuce, shredded
¼ small cucumber, chopped
2 tablespoons low-calorie dressing (page 8)
8 thin slices of boiled ham
1 pickled cucumber, cut into 8 strips

Spread cut sides of baps with mustard. Mix lettuce, cucumber and dressing. Put equal amounts of salad on to each slice of ham and add a cucumber strip. Roll each up like a baby Swiss roll, and place two rolls inside each bap. Makes 4.

Cucumber Sandwiches

106 calories per serving

3 tablespoons vinegar
2 tablespoons water
1 teaspoon sugar
¼ teaspoon salt
¼ teaspoon dill
Dash of pepper
1 large unpeeled cucumber, thinly sliced
4 slices of white bread
1 oz (25 gm) butter
4 radishes, thinly sliced

Combine vinegar, water, sugar, salt, dill and pepper; add sliced cucumber. Cover and chill for 3 hours, stirring occasionally. Drain. Top buttered bread with cucumber and radishes. Makes 4.

Choose from, top to bottom, Fruit Wheel, Cucumber Sandwich, Open Chicken Sandwich, Ham and Salad Roll or Cottage Cheese Surprise for a light and satisfying lunch.

48

LOW-CALORIE

COOKING TIP

*Sandwiches are
an easy low-calorie
lunch or snack*

Serve sandwiches open to eliminate a second bread slice. Lightly spread bread with softened or whipped butter or margarine. (Softened or whipped butter spreads easily, so less is needed than with firm spreads.) Top bread with remaining sandwich ingredients.

Tuna Salad Sandwich

157 calories per serving

1 can (7½ oz or 185 gm) tuna, drained and flaked
3 oz (75 gm) cottage cheese
1 medium celery stalk, chopped
1 tablespoon chopped sweet pickle
1 tablespoon chopped onion
1 tablespoon low-calorie dressing (page 8)
¼ teaspoon salt
4 slices of rye bread
4 teaspoons mayonnaise
4 lettuce leaves
4 slices of tomato

Mix together first seven ingredients. Spread each slice of bread with 1 teaspoon mayonnaise, and top with a lettuce leaf and a slice of tomato. Sprinkle with salt, and spoon tuna mixture on top of tomatoes. Makes 4.

Salmon Sandwich

146 calories per serving

Pink salmon has fewer calories than red salmon

1 can (7½ oz or 185 gm) pink salmon, drained and flaked
4 tablespoons low-calorie dressing (page 8)
1 small can water chestnuts, drained and finely chopped
1 tablespoon sliced onion
1 teaspoon Soy sauce
1 teaspoon lemon juice
6 slices of rye bread
6 small tomatoes

In a bowl combine first six ingredients and mix thoroughly. Spread salmon mixture on bread slices, garnish each with tomato, and serve open. Makes 6.

Shrimp Stack-ups

156 calories per serving

8 oz (200 gm) peeled shrimps, chopped
1 tablespoon lemon juice
1 large celery stalk, chopped
2 tablespoons chopped sweet pickle
2 tablespoons thinly sliced onion
¼ teaspoon salt
Dash of pepper
4 tablespoons low-calorie dressing (page 8)
3 bap rolls, split and toasted
6 lettuce leaves
6 slices of tomato
1 hard-boiled egg, sliced

In a small bowl sprinkle shrimps with lemon juice, and add celery, sweet pickle, onion, salt, pepper and dressing. Mix gently, then chill. Top each bap half with a lettuce leaf and tomato slice. Spoon equal amounts of shrimp mixture on top of each. Garnish with egg slices. Makes 6.

Crab Grill Deluxe

139 calories per serving

8 oz (200 gm) crab meat, flaked
3 tablespoons low-calorie dressing (page 8)
1 oz (25 gm) processed cheese, grated
1 medium celery stalk, finely chopped
1 tablespoon chopped canned pimiento
2 teaspoons lemon juice
3 bap rolls, split and toasted
Parsley (optional)

In a bowl combine crab, dressing, cheese, celery, pimiento and lemon juice; mix well. Spread equal amounts of the crab mixture on top of each bap half. Grill 4 to 5 inches from heat till cheese melts, about 2 to 3 minutes. Garnish with parsley, if liked. Makes 6.

Devilled Hamburgers

251 calories per serving

1 beaten egg
4 tablespoons skimmed milk
1 oz (25 gm) fresh white breadcrumbs
½ small green pepper, chopped
8 oz (200 gm) lean ham, finely chopped
1 oz (25 gm) butter
3 bap rolls, split and toasted
Cucumber slices
Small radishes

HORSERADISH SAUCE:
1 oz (25 gm) butter
1 oz (25 gm) flour
½ pint (250 ml) skimmed milk
1 teaspoon prepared horseradish
1 teaspoon prepared mustard
¼ teaspoon salt

In a bowl combine egg, skimmed milk, breadcrumbs and green pepper. Add ham and mix well. Shape into six patties. Brown on both sides in butter, and stand a patty on each bap half. Garnish with cucumber slices and radishes. Makes 6.

Serve with hot **Horseradish Sauce**. Melt butter in a saucepan and stir in flour. Blend in skimmed milk, and cook, stirring, till thick and bubbly. Remove from heat, and stir in horseradish, mustard and salt.

Hot Cheese-egg Sandwich

185 calories per serving

4 hard-boiled eggs, chopped
3 tablespoons low-calorie dressing
  (page 8)
2 tablespoons sweet pickle relish
2 tablespoons chopped onion
1 tablespoon prepared mustard
6 slices of white bread, toasted
4 oz (100 gm) Mozzarella cheese, sliced
6 slices of tomato
Salt

In a medium bowl combine eggs, dressing, sweet pickle relish, onion and mustard. Spread on bread, and grill 4 inches from heat till heated through, about 3 to 4 minutes. Cover sandwiches with cheese and top each with a tomato slice, then sprinkle with salt. Return to grill till cheese melts. Makes 6.

Open Beefburgers

232 calories per serving

4 slices of rye bread
½ lb (200 gm) lean minced beef
Salt
4 thin slices of onion
8 thin slices of tomato
3 oz (75 gm) Mozzarella cheese, sliced

Toast bread on one side. Divide beef and spread to edges on untoasted side of bread. Sprinkle with salt. Grill 3 inches from heat for 5 to 6 minutes. Top each sandwich with an onion slice and two tomato slices. Grill for 2 minutes more, cover with cheese and grill till it melts. Makes 4.

Ham-asparagus Grill

184 calories per serving

1 medium can asparagus spears
4 slices of white bread, toasted
2 teaspoons prepared mustard
4 slices of boiled ham
2 oz (50 gm) processed cheese, grated
2 tablespoons chopped onion
1 tablespoon chopped canned pimiento

Heat asparagus, drain and keep warm. Spread mustard on one side of toast. Cover each with a ham slice, then arrange hot asparagus spears on top. Combine remaining ingredients and sprinkle on top of asparagus. Grill 5 inches from heat till cheese melts, about 2 to 3 minutes. Makes 4.

Cottage Cheese Surprise

145 calories per serving

12 oz (300 gm) cottage cheese
2 medium celery stalks, chopped
1 medium carrot, grated
8 large radishes, chopped
½ teaspoon caraway seed
6 slices of thinly sliced white bread
1 oz (25 gm) butter, softened
6 lettuce leaves

Mash cheese with a fork, and stir in celery, carrot, radishes and caraway seed. Chill. Top buttered bread with lettuce. Spread sandwiches with equal amounts of the cheese mixture. Makes 6.

Light and Satisfying Desserts

Lemon-blackcurrant Fluff

76 calories per serving

1 lemon-flavoured jelly
¼ pint (125 ml) boiling water
Cold water
¼ teaspoon grated lemon peel
2 tablespoons lemon juice
2 egg whites
8 oz (200 gm) blackcurrants, fresh if
   possible
1 tablespoon cornflour
4 tablespoons cold water
Few drops of vanilla essence
Liquid artificial sweetener to taste

In a large bowl dissolve jelly in boiling water. Make up to ¾ pint (375 ml) with cold water. Stir in lemon peel and juice. Chill till partially set. Add unbeaten egg whites to jelly mixture, and beat with an electric mixer till mixture is light and fluffy, about 1 to 2 minutes. Pour into eight dariole moulds and chill till firm. (Slight separation into layers may occur.)

Meanwhile, in a saucepan crush a third of the blackcurrants. Blend together cornflour and cold water, and add to crushed currants. Cook over medium heat, stirring constantly, till mixture is thick and bubbly; cook and stir for 1 minute longer. Remove sauce from heat and stir in remaining currants and vanilla essence. Sweeten and chill.

To serve, unmould lemon fluff in individual dessert dishes. Spoon a little sauce over each dessert. Serves 8.

Yogurt-fruit Medley

86 calories per serving

1 medium can pineapple chunks
2 teaspoons sugar

Topped with a fresh flavoured blackcurrant sauce, Lemon-blackcurrant Fluff is sure to tempt both dieters and non-dieters.

2 teaspoons cornflour
½ teaspoon vanilla essence
¼ pint (125 ml) natural yogurt
3 medium oranges, peeled, sectioned
   and coarsely chopped
4 oz (100 gm) seedless grapes, halved

Drain pineapple chunks, reserving juice. In a saucepan blend sugar with cornflour and stir in reserved juice. Cook, stirring, over medium heat till thick and bubbly. Reduce heat, then cook and stir for 1 minute more. Remove from heat and stir in vanilla essence. Cool for 10 minutes without stirring. Blend mixture into yogurt and add pineapple, oranges and grapes. Mix lightly, then chill. Serves 8.

Rhubarb and Strawberry Bowl

56 calories per serving

¾ lb (300 gm) fresh rhubarb, cut into 1
   inch slices
4 tablespoons sugar
1 breakfast cup+3 tablespoons cold
   water
1 tablespoon cornflour
Dash of salt
1 teaspoon lemon juice
Few drops of red food colouring
12 oz (200 gm) fresh strawberries, sliced

In a saucepan combine rhubarb, sugar and 1 breakfast cup water. Bring to boil and reduce heat. Simmer till almost tender, about 2 minutes. Remove from heat and drain, reserving syrup. Add water to syrup to make ½ pint (250 ml). Mix cornflour, salt and 3 tablespoons cold water, and add to syrup mixture. Cook and stir till thick and bubbly, then cook and stir for 2 minutes more. Remove from heat and cool slightly. Stir in lemon juice and food colouring, then gently stir in rhubarb and strawberries. Chill. Serves 8.

Raspberry-yogurt Fluff

74 calories per serving

1 packet (10 oz or 250 gm) frozen
    raspberries
1 tablespoon cornflour
½ pint (250 ml) natural yogurt
¼ teaspoon almond essence
Few drops of red food colouring
1 egg white
¼ teaspoon cream of tartar

Thaw raspberries and drain, reserving syrup. Add water to syrup to make ½ pint (250 ml). In a saucepan blend syrup mixture with cornflour. Cook, stirring over medium heat till thick and bubbly. Remove from heat and cool. Stir in yogurt, almond essence and food colouring, then fold in raspberries. Beat egg white with cream of tartar till stiff peaks form. Gently fold into yogurt mixture. Spoon into dessert dishes and chill. Serves 6.

Grapefruit and Raspberry Compôte

89 calories per serving

1 packet (10 oz or 250 gm) frozen
    raspberries
3 tablespoons water
2 tablespoons sugar
3 inch stick cinnamon
½ teaspoon whole cloves
2 large grapefruit

Thaw raspberries and drain, reserving syrup. Mix syrup, water, sugar, cinnamon and cloves. Bring to boil and reduce heat. Simmer, uncovered, for 10 minutes, then strain. Peel and section grapefruit and place in a shallow serving dish. Top with raspberries, and pour syrup over fruit. Cover, then chill for several hours or overnight. Serves 6.

Strawberry-melon Parfaits

80 calories per serving

1 lb (½ kilo) fresh strawberries
1 tablespoon+2 teaspoons sugar
1 large ripe banana, mashed
¼ pint (125 ml) natural yogurt
⅛ teaspoon cinnamon
½ medium melon, diced

Reserve six strawberries, quarter remainder and sprinkle with 1 tablespoon sugar. Mix banana, yogurt, cinnamon and 2 teaspoons sugar, blending well. Arrange melon in the bottom of six sundae glasses, and spoon half the banana mixture over melon. Top with sweetened strawberries, and spoon remaining banana mixture over them. Garnish with reserved whole strawberries. Serves 6.

Apple-ginger Bake

113 calories per serving

5 apples, peeled, cored and sliced
8 gingersnaps, crushed
2 tablespoons brown sugar
4 tablespoons water
1 tablespoon lemon juice

Place half the apples in the bottom of a baking dish, 2 inches deep, and about 8 by 8 inches. Mix gingersnap crumbs and brown sugar. Sprinkle half the crumb mixture over apple slices. Top with remaining apples and sprinkle with remaining crumbs. Mix water and lemon juice, and pour evenly over apple mixture. Bake, covered, at Gas No 5 or 375°F (191°C) till apples are tender, about 40 to 45 minutes. Serve warm. Serves 6.

Raspberry Ice

90 calories per serving

2 packets (each 10 oz or 250 gm) frozen
    raspberries
1 raspberry-flavoured jelly
¼ pint (125 ml) boiling water
4 tablespoons fresh orange juice
1 tablespoon lemon juice

Thaw raspberries, sieve and set aside. Dissolve jelly in boiling water. Add orange juice and make up to ¾ pint (375 ml) with cold water. Add lemon juice, then stir in sieved raspberries. Freeze in two empty ice cube trays until mixture is firm. Break into chunks and in a chilled bowl beat half the mixture with an electric beater till smooth. Return to tray, and repeat with remaining mixture. Freeze till firm. Serves 10.

Raspberry-apple Dessert

67 calories per serving

- 1 raspberry-flavoured jelly
- ½ pint (250 ml) boiling water
- ½ pint (250 ml) unsweetened apple purée made from stewed apples
- 2 egg whites
- Dash of salt
- 8 teaspoons desiccated coconut (optional)

Dissolve jelly in boiling water. Stir in apple purée and chill till mixture is partially set. Beat egg whites with salt till soft peaks form. Fold into jelly mixture. Chill, if necessary, till mixture mounds and spoon into sundae glasses. If liked, sprinkle each serving with 1 teaspoon desiccated coconut. Serves 8.

SEASONING GUIDE FOR FRUITS

Spices and flavourings add variety to fresh fruit, baked fruit desserts and compôtes without increasing calories. Experiment with different spices and flavourings by adding a small amount to individual fruits or fruit mixtures. Or use ground spices as a garnish and sprinkle lightly over fruit or baked desserts before serving.

Apples	allspice, caraway seed, cardamom, cinnamon, cloves, dill, ginger, mint, nutmeg, almond extract, citrus flavourings
Bananas	allspice, cinnamon, ginger, nutmeg
Berries (Strawberries, Raspberries etc)	cinnamon, cloves, ginger, nutmeg, rosemary, vanilla essence
Cherries	allspice, cloves, cinnamon, mace, mint, nutmeg, almond essence, brandy essence, rum essence, vanilla essence
Cranberries	allspice, cinnamon, cloves, ginger, nutmeg, rosemary, almond essence
Grapefruit	cinnamon, ginger
Grapes	allspice, cinnamon, cloves
Melons	cardamom, ginger, mint
Oranges	allspice, anise, cinnamon, cloves, ginger, mace, nutmeg, rosemary
Peaches	allspice, cinnamon, cloves, ginger, nutmeg, rosemary, almond essence, brandy essence, rum essence
Pears	allspice, anise, cinnamon, mint, nutmeg
Pineapple	allspice, cardamom, cinnamon, cloves, coriander, mace, mint, nutmeg, rosemary, vanilla essence
Plums	allspice, cinnamon, cloves, almond essence
Prunes	allspice, anise, cinnamon, cloves, ginger, nutmeg, almond essence, citrus flavourings
Rhubarb	cinnamon, ginger, nutmeg, rosemary, citrus flavourings, vanilla essence

Baked Crimson Pears

69 calories per serving

4 fresh medium pears
½ pint (250 ml) apple juice
3 inch stick cinnamon
Red food colouring

Peel, halve and core pears, and place in 2 pint casserole. Mix apple juice and cinnamon. Colour deep pink with food colouring, then bring to boil. Pour over pears. Bake, covered, at Gas No 4 or 350°F (177°C) for 10 minutes. Turn pears and bake, covered, for 10 minutes more. Turn pears again and bake, uncovered, till tender, a further 5 to 10 minutes. Remove cinnamon stick and serve in juice. Serves 8.

Rosy red pears with vitamin-filled apple juice make up this eye-catching dessert, Baked Crimson Pears.

Pineapple Dessert

79 calories per serving

1 large can crushed pineapple
1 envelope (about 3 teaspoons) gelatine
1 oz (25 gm) sugar
¼ teaspoon vanilla essence
Red or green food colouring
½ oz (12 gm) instant low-fat milk
   granules
4 tablespoons iced water

Thoroughly drain pineapple. Reserve syrup and make up to ½ pint (250 ml) with cold water (if necessary). Pour into a saucepan, and add gelatine and sugar. Stir over low heat till both have dissolved. Remove from heat and stir in vanilla essence, several drops of red or green food colouring and the pineapple. Chill till partially set. In a mixing bowl combine milk granules with iced water. Beat at high speed until stiff peaks form. Carefully fold in gelatine mixture, then chill, if necessary, till mixture mounds. Spoon into sundae glasses, and chill till firm. Serves 8.

Baked Orange Cups

107 calories per serving

4 medium oranges
3 oz (75 gm) seedless green grapes,
   halved
Dash of bitters
2 tablespoons desiccated coconut

Remove tops of oranges and, with a grapefruit knife, scoop out pulp and reserve. Dice reserved pulp and toss with halved grapes and bitters. Spoon fruit into orange shells. Place in a shallow baking dish. Pour a little water around oranges, and bake at Gas No 3 or 325°F (163°C) for 25 minutes. Sprinkle with desiccated coconut, then bake for 8 to 10 minutes more. Serves 4.

Snow Pudding

132 calories per serving

2½ oz (62 gm) caster sugar
⅛ teaspoon salt
2 teaspoons gelatine
7 tablespoons cold water
¼ teaspoon grated lemon peel
2 tablespoons lemon juice
2 egg whites
Diabetic red jam

CUSTARD SAUCE:
¼ pint (125 ml) skimmed milk
2 egg yolks
4 teaspoons sugar
Dash of salt
½ teaspoon vanilla essence

In a saucepan combine caster sugar, salt and gelatine. Add 4 tablespoons cold water and stir over low heat to dissolve. Remove from heat and add 3 tablespoons cold water, lemon peel and lemon juice. Chill till partially set. Turn into a bowl and add unbeaten egg whites. Beat with electric or rotary beater till the mixture begins to hold its shape. Pour into five dariole moulds and chill till firm. To serve, unmould, coat with Custard Sauce and top with diabetic red jam. Serves 5.

Custard Sauce: In a heavy saucepan combine skimmed milk, beaten egg yolks, sugar and salt. Cook, stirring, over very low heat till the mixture coats a metal spoon. Remove from heat and cool immediately by placing pan in cold water. Stir for several minutes, then stir in vanilla essence. Chill.

Spoonfuls of red jam add the crowning touch to Snow Pudding. Mound the puddings in a colourful glass bowl or serve individually.

LOW-CALORIE

COOKING TIP

Use a refrigerator tray to freeze low-calorie ices. When the mixture is frozen, break into chunks with a fork. For whipped ices, transfer chunks to chilled bowl and beat till smooth. Return to tray and freeze till firm.

Glorified Rice

98 calories per serving

 ¼ pint (125 ml) water
 1 packet (2 oz or 50 gm) quick cooking
   long grain rice
 ¼ teaspoon salt
 1 large can crushed pineapple
 1 medium banana, sliced
 2 teaspoons lemon juice
 ¼ pint (125 ml) natural yogurt
 1 tablespoon sugar
 1 teaspoon vanilla essence
 ½ lb (200 gm) strawberries, halved

In a saucepan combine water, rice and salt; stir to moisten. Bring to boil, then cover and simmer for 5 minutes. Remove from heat and leave to stand for 5 minutes. Stir in drained pineapple and cool. Meanwhile, sprinkle banana with lemon juice. Stir banana slices into cooled rice mixture. Combine yogurt, sugar and essence, and fold into rice mixture. Chill. Spoon rice mixture into a serving dish and top with strawberries. Serves 8.

Marinated Fruit

85 calories per serving

 1 large can (1 lb or ½ kilo) pineapple
   chunks
 1 medium apple
 1 fresh medium pear
 1 medium nectarine or peach
 2 tablespoons orange juice
 1 tablespoon honey
 1 teaspoon chopped fresh mint

Drain pineapple, reserving juice. Remove cores from unpeeled apple and pear, and stone nectarine or peach. Cut fruit into chunks, and mix in a shallow dish. Mix reserved juice with remaining ingredients, then pour over fruit. Stir to mix. Cover and marinate in the refrigerator for 2 to 3 hours, stirring occasionally. Serve with marinade. Serves 8.

Peachy Orange Ice

74 calories per serving

 4 ripe peaches, peeled and sliced
 ½ pint (250 ml) fresh orange juice
 1 tablespoon lemon juice
 3 egg whites
 Dash of salt
 3 tablespoons caster sugar

In a blender goblet combine peaches, orange juice and lemon juice, then blend till peaches are puréed, about 15 seconds. Beat egg whites with salt till soft peaks form. Gradually add sugar, beating till stiff peaks form. Transfer peach purée to a mixing bowl and gently fold in beaten egg whites. Freeze peach mixture in two empty ice cube trays till mixture is almost firm. Remove to a chilled bowl and beat well with rotary or electric beater. Return to freezer trays and freeze till mixture is firm. To serve, spoon frozen peach mixture into sundae dishes. Serves 8.

Spicy Peach Compôte

63 calories per serving

 3 large fresh peaches
 Lemon juice
 2 teaspoons cornflour
 2 tablespoons sugar
 ¼ teaspoon salt
 4 tablespoons fresh orange juice
 ¼ pint (125 ml) water
 ½ teaspoon grated orange peel
 4 inch stick cinnamon
 5 whole cloves

Peel and halve peaches, remove stones, and sprinkle with lemon juice to prevent darkening. In a saucepan mix cornflour, sugar and salt. Stir in all remaining ingredients. Cook, stirring, till thick and bubbly, then cook, stirring, for 2 minutes more. Pour hot mixture over peaches and chill. Remove spices before serving. Serves 6.

*Use skimmed milk in
cooking and as a drink*

Substitute skimmed milk (prepared from low-fat
instant milk granules) for whole milk—it is rich in
protein and contains about half the calories.

Raspberry Bavarian Mould

60 calories per serving

1 packet (10 oz or 250 gm) frozen
   raspberries
1 envelope (about 3 teaspoons) gelatine
¼ pint (125 ml) boiling water
¼ pint (125 ml) cold water
1 tablespoon lemon juice
Dash of salt
¼ pint (125 ml) evaporated milk, chilled

Thaw raspberries, reserving 2 tablespoons for
garnish. Drain remaining raspberries, reserving 6
tablespoons syrup. Dissolve gelatine in boiling
water. Stir in cold water, reserved syrup, lemon
juice and salt. Chill till mixture is partially set, then
add evaporated milk. Beat at high speed with an
electric mixer till soft peaks form, about 4 minutes.
Fold in drained raspberries and pour into a 3 pint
mould. Chill till firm, about 2 to 3 hours. Unmould
and decorate with reserved raspberries. Serves 8.

Lemon Snow

80 calories per serving

1 envelope (about 3 teaspoons) gelatine
2 oz (50 gm) sugar
¼ teaspoon salt
½ pint (250 ml) cold water
¼ pint (125 ml) lemon juice
½ teaspoon grated lemon peel
2 egg whites
2–3 drops green food colouring

In a saucepan combine gelatine, sugar and salt.
Stir in cold water, and stir over low heat till gelatine
is dissolved. Remove from heat and add lemon
juice and lemon peel. Chill till partially set, then
turn into a large bowl. Add unbeaten egg whites

and green food colouring. Beat at high speed with
an electric mixer till light and fluffy, about 1 to 2
minutes. Pour into a 2½ pint mould and chill till
firm. Serves 8.

Meringue-topped Peaches

97 calories per serving

1 large can (1 lb or ½ kilo) or 2 small cans
   diabetic peach slices, drained
2 tablespoons orange juice
½ teaspoon grated lemon peel
2 egg whites
¼ teaspoon salt
¼ teaspoon vanilla essence
1 tablespoon sugar
Custard Sauce (page 55)

Place peaches in a shallow baking dish. Spoon
orange juice and lemon peel over peaches. Beat
egg whites with salt and essence till soft peaks
form. Gradually add sugar and beat till stiff peaks
form. Swirl meringue over peaches. Bake at Gas
No 6 or 400°F (204°C) till just browned, about 7
minutes. Spoon Custard Sauce over. Serves 6.

Mocha Chiffon

104 calories per serving

4 oz (100 gm) sugar
2 envelopes (about 6 teaspoons) gelatine
2 tablespoons cocoa powder
1 tablespoon instant coffee granules
½ teaspoon salt
1 pint (½ litre) skimmed milk
6 tablespoons water
3 eggs, separated
1 teaspoon vanilla essence
¼ teaspoon cream of tartar
Crushed biscuit crumbs

In a saucepan mix sugar, gelatine, cocoa, coffee
and salt. Combine skimmed milk, water and beaten
egg yolks. Stir milk mixture into gelatine mixture.
Cook over medium heat, stirring constantly, till
gelatine and sugar dissolve and mixture thickens
slightly. Remove from heat and chill mixture till
partially set. Beat together egg whites, essence
and cream of tartar till soft peaks form. Carefully
fold gelatine mixture into egg whites. Chill till
mixture mounds, then spoon into 3 pint mould and
chill till firm. To serve, unmould dessert on to a
plate. Sprinkle with biscuit crumbs. Serves 10.

Streamlined Beverages

Apricot-pineapple Frost

61 calories per serving

1 can (1 lb or ½ kilo) apricots
¼ pint (125 ml) pineapple juice, chilled
½ teaspoon peppermint essence
Mint sprigs (optional)

In a liquidiser goblet combine apricots, pineapple juice and peppermint. Cover and blend for a few seconds, until frothy. Pour over ice in glasses and garnish with mint sprigs, if liked. Serves 5–6.

Strawberry Shake

72 calories per serving

¾ pint (375 ml) skimmed milk, chilled
2 tablespoons sugar
Dash of ground cinnamon
1 lb (½ kilo) fresh or frozen unsweetened strawberries

In a liquidiser goblet combine milk, sugar and cinnamon; gradually add strawberries. Blend on medium speed till smooth. Serve immediately. Serves 5.

Citrus Cooler

50 calories per serving

1 can frozen grapefruit or orange juice, thawed
¾ pint (375 ml) cold water
Dash of bitters
1 bottle low-calorie bitter lemon

In a jug combine grapefruit or orange juice, cold water and bitters; chill thoroughly. Just before serving, carefully pour bitter lemon down side of the jug and stir gently with an up-and-down motion. Serve over ice. Serves 6.

Apple and Apricot Cooler

61 calories per serving

¾ pint (375 ml) apple juice
1 can (1 lb or ½ kilo) apricots
3 tablespoons lemon juice
¼ teaspoon bitters
1 pint (½ litre) soda water, chilled
8 thin slices of lemon

Put apple juice into a large jug. Blend apricots with syrup in a liquidiser goblet until smooth. Add to apple juice in jug, and stir in lemon juice and bitters. Just before serving, carefully pour soda water down side of the jug, stirring gently with an up-and-down motion. Serve over ice in glasses and garnish with lemon slices. Serves 8.

Raspberry Fizz

48 calories per serving

¾ pint (375 ml) pineapple juice, chilled
1 packet (10 oz or 250 gm) frozen raspberries, thawed
¼ pint (125 ml) water
4 bottles low-calorie bitter lemon, chilled
Mint sprigs

In a liquidiser goblet combine pineapple juice, raspberries and water. Blend on medium speed till raspberries are puréed, then strain. Pour mixture into a jug. Gradually pour bitter lemon down side of the jug, stirring with an up-and-down motion. Serve over ice and garnish with mint sprigs. Serves 10.

Blend Apricot-pineapple Frost till a big frothy head appears. Pour into tall tumblers over ice and garnish with mint sprigs.

Serve Ruby Lemonade Punch in a large punchbowl at your next get-together. Float thin lemon slices on top.

Orange Frost

48 calories per serving

1 can frozen orange juice concentrate, thawed
6 teacups finely crushed ice

Place orange juice in a chilled liquidiser goblet. Add ice, 1 cup at a time, blending well after each addition. Stop blender several times and push ice down with a rubber spatula. Serve in tall glasses with straws and spoons. Serves 6.

Orange and Lemon Cooler

41 calories per serving

4 bottles low-calorie bitter lemon
1 can frozen orange juice concentrate, thawed
Mint sprigs

Pour bitter lemon into freezer trays or a shallow pan, and freeze firm. Break into chunks and crush. Pour orange juice into liquidiser goblet and add frozen crushed bitter lemon, a little at a time, blending well after each addition. Stop blender several times and push ice down with a rubber spatula. Spoon into glasses and garnish with mint sprigs. Serves 8.

Ruby Lemonade Punch

74 calories per serving

1 can frozen orange juice concentrate, thawed
1½ pints (¾ litre) tomato juice
2 bottles low-calorie bitter lemon

Stir orange juice into tomato juice. Slowly add bitter lemon and stir gently with an up-and-down motion. Serve over ice and garnish with lemon slices. Serves 8.

Grape and Grapefruit Punch

49 calories per serving

¾ pint (375 ml) grapefruit juice, chilled
¾ pint (375 ml) grape juice, chilled
1 pint (½ litre) soda water
Slices of lemon (optional)

Combine grapefruit juice and grape juice, and chill. Just before serving, slowly add soda water, stirring with an up-and-down motion. Garnish with lemon slices, if liked. Serves 10.

Fruity Orange Tea

59 calories per serving

4 teaspoons instant tea powder
1 pint (½ litre) cold water
½ can frozen orange juice concentrate, thawed
½ pint (250 ml) pineapple juice
Few drops of green food colouring
Mint sprigs

In a jug dissolve instant tea powder in cold water. Stir in orange juice, pineapple juice and green food colouring. Chill, and serve over ice in glasses. Garnish with mint sprigs, if liked. Serves 6.

Spiced Iced Coffee

63 calories per serving

¾ pint (375 ml) skimmed milk
2 tablespoons sugar
2 tablespoons instant coffee granules
½ teaspoon mixed spice
2 bottles low-calorie ginger ale, chilled

In a liquidiser goblet combine skimmed milk, sugar, coffee and mixed spice; blend till well mixed. Just before serving, carefully add ginger ale, stirring gently with an up-and-down motion. Serve over ice. Serves 6.

Mulled Apple Drink

66 calories per serving

1½ pints (¾ litre) apple juice
1 pint (½ litre) pineapple juice
1 teaspoon whole allspice
1 teaspoon whole cloves
Dash of salt
Dash of ground nutmeg
3 inch stick cinnamon

In a large saucepan combine all ingredients and slowly bring to boil. Reduce heat, cover and simmer for 20 minutes. Remove from heat and pour juice mixture through a strainer to remove whole spices. Serves 8.

Hot Spiced Tea

77 calories per serving

1 pint (½ litre) pineapple juice
¾ pint (375 ml) orange juice
¾ pint (375 ml) water
4 teaspoons instant tea powder
1 teaspoon whole allspice
3 inch stick cinnamon

Put all ingredients into a saucepan. Bring to boil, reduce heat and simmer, covered, for 15 minutes. Strain. Serves 8.

Vanilla-coffee Skimmer

77 calories per serving

2 teaspoons instant coffee granules
1½ pints(¾ litre) skimmed milk
2 tablespoons sugar
1 teaspoon vanilla essence
Coffee Ice Cubes

Dissolve coffee powder in skimmed milk. Add sugar and vanilla essence, and stir. Serve over Coffee Ice Cubes. Serves 5.

Coffee Ice Cubes: Stir together 2 teaspoons instant coffee granules for each ¾ pint (375 ml) water. Freeze in ice cube trays.

LOW-CALORIE

COOKING TIP

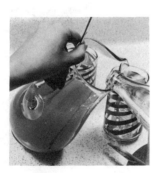

Reduce calories in punches and fruit drinks by using low-calorie carbonated drinks. Just before serving, carefully pour carbonated drinks down the inside of the jug. Stir gently with an up-and-down motion.

Float frozen Coffee Ice Cubes on top of Vanilla-coffee Skimmer, to add drinking enjoyment.

Calorie-planned Menus

Need help in planning a sensible weight control programme? Then learn the simplified method for determining calorie needs. Once you've got this under way, use the Basic Four Menu Guide to plan your daily menus. Or, follow our weekly menu plan that is tailored to your calorie needs and designed with flavour, appetite appeal and nutrition in mind. You'll soon discover how to calorie-count and enjoy it.

Inviting entrées, such as Green Pepper Steak, served with Fluffy Rice, lettuce wedge and fruit, make appealing and satisfying diet fare.

How to Plan Low-calorie Menus

A well-balanced diet is important regardless of whether the ultimate goal is to lose a few pounds or to maintain your present weight. Too often the chief concern of the overweight individual is that of reducing calories without regard for adequate nutrition. However, calories should not be lowered indiscriminately. The diet must still provide the essential nutrients for the body.

An overweight condition is most often the result of taking in more calories than the body needs. Likewise, a weight loss generally results when the calorific intake is lower than the calorific need. To balance these two factors, you must first know the number of calories required by the body. These needs are based upon your age, desirable weight, and the amount of your daily physical activity. Use the simplified method for working out your daily calorific needs (see below). Once this is known, you can work out a diet.

For example, approximately 3500 calories are needed to make 1 lb ($\frac{1}{2}$ kilo) of fat body tissue. If the calorific intake is reduced by 500 calories per day (3500 per week), approximately 1 pound ($\frac{1}{2}$ kilo) per week is lost. By lowering the daily calorific intake 1000 calories (7000 calories per week), weight loss is increased to about 2 pounds (1 kilo) per week. It is important to note, however, that weight loss may vary slightly depending upon the particular individual. Two pounds per week is about the maximum weight loss most doctors recommend, unless the individual is under a specific medically supervised programme.

But it's not simply a matter of consuming a set number of calories. You must also balance your diet nutritionally. To do this, each day's menus should provide the number of servings recommended by the Basic Four. To check this, use the Basic Four Menu Guide (see page 65) for planning your menus. Select foods from each group which are relatively low in calories. However, if the daily calorific allowance is quite low, it is not always possible to include the total recommended number of servings from the Bread-Cereal Group in the Basic Four.

To plan a lunch or dinner menu, select a main dish from the Meat Group which provides one serving for each family member. (The breakfast menu may or may not include a main dish.) Add a vegetable, salad, bread, dessert and drink which complement the main dish in flavour, texture and colour. Avoid food preparation methods such as frying or sautéeing which tend to add calories. Instead, prepare food by grilling, roasting, poaching or steaming. When possible, serve fruit and vegetables raw to keep calories low.

Use the calorie-counted menus (see pages 66–73) as a guide for planning your menus. Note that the breakfast menu often provides fewer calories than either lunch or dinner. However, this pattern can be adjusted, depending upon personal preference. Remember: serving portions must be controlled for an effective diet. A wider variety of foods which are nutritionally sound are possible when menus are planned in advance.

To Calculate Calorific Needs

Estimate desirable weight for your height in pounds by consulting a weight chart.

Multiply your desirable weight by the number 16 if you are a woman and 18 if you are a man. (These numbers are based on a light amount of physical activity. Additional calories will be needed by those who regularly engage in strenuous physical activities. Since many people tend to overestimate their energy requirements, the above figures are a satisfactory guide for most people in their daily routine.)

Subtract 10 calories for each year of age over 22. (Desired weight at age 22 should be maintained throughout life. As you grow older, fewer calories are needed to maintain weight.)

Basic Four Menu Guide

Milk Group—¾–1½ pints (375 ml–¾ litre) daily

Includes milk, buttermilk, yogurt, ice cream and cheese.

Recommended allowances:
- ¾–1 pint (375 ml–½ litre) for children
- 1½ pints (¾ litre) or more for teenagers
- ¾ pint (375 ml) or more for adults

Calcium equivalents for 8 fluid oz (200 gm or ⅖ pint) milk:
- 1¾ oz (33 gm) Cheddar-type cheese
- 12 oz (300 gm) cottage cheese
- ¾ pint (375 ml) ice cream

Meat Group—2 servings daily

Includes beef, veal, pork, lamb, poultry, fish and eggs. Alternative sources of protein include dried beans, dried peas, nuts and peanut butter.

Consider as one serving:
- 2–3 oz (50–75 gm) cooked meat, fish or poultry
- 2 eggs
- 1 breakfast cup cooked dried beans, peas or lentils
- 4 tablespoons peanut butter

Vegetable-Fruit Group—4 servings daily

Include one serving of citrus fruit or tomatoes daily and one serving of a dark green leafy vegetable, deep yellow vegetable, or yellow fruit (fresh peaches or apricots) 3 to 4 times a week.

Consider as one serving:
- 4 oz (100 gm) vegetables or fruit
- 1 medium apple, banana or potato
- ½ grapefruit or medium slice of melon

Bread-Cereal Group—4 servings daily

Includes breads, cereals, cream crackers, pasta, rice and semolina.

Consider as 1 serving:
- 1 slice of bread
- 1 teacup to 1 breakfast cup ready-to-eat cereal
- 2–3 oz (50 to 75 gm) cooked cereal, rice, macaroni, noodles or spaghetti

Select foods for a balanced diet from the Milk Group and Meat Group, left, which include cheese, ice-cream, poultry and eggs, and the nutritious Vegetable-Fruit and Bread-Cereal Groups, below.

1000 Calorie Menus

Day 1

BREAKFAST—*206 calories*

¼ pint (125 ml) orange juice
½ teacup crisp rice cereal
3 tablespoons skimmed milk
1 teaspoon sugar
1 boiled egg
Coffee or tea

LUNCH—*306 calories*

Salmon Sandwich*
Average portion of lettuce
1 tablespoon low-calorie dressing
3 oz (75 gm) green grapes
¼ pint (125 ml) skimmed milk
Coffee or tea

DINNER—*498 calories*

Liver with Mushrooms*
Sesame Broccoli*
Carrot and Orange Salad*
Pineapple Dessert*
8 fluid oz (200 ml) skimmed milk
Coffee or tea

Day 4

BREAKFAST—*204 calories*

4 oz (100 gm) fresh strawberries
1 breakfast cup rice cereal
¼ pint (125 ml) skimmed milk
1 teaspoon sugar
Coffee or tea

LUNCH—*360 calories*

3 oz (75 gm) lean beef hamburger
½ bap roll
1 teaspoon ketchup or mustard
Average portion of lettuce
1 tablespoon low-calorie dressing
Lemon-blackcurrant Fluff*
¼ pint (125 ml) skimmed milk
Coffee or tea

DINNER—*448 calories*

Seafood Divan*
4 oz (100 gm) cottage cheese
½ medium fresh peach on a lettuce leaf
Grapefruit and Raspberry Compôte*
8 fluid oz (200 ml) skimmed milk
Coffee or tea

Day 5

BREAKFAST—*222 calories*

¼ pint (125 ml) grapefruit juice
½ breakfast cup wheat cereal
3 tablespoons skimmed milk
1 teaspoon sugar
1 boiled egg
Coffee or tea

LUNCH—*275 calories*

Prawn-stuffed Tomato*
Spicy Peach Compôte*
8 fluid oz (200 ml) skimmed milk
Coffee or tea

DINNER—*516 calories*

Hawaiian Ham Slice*
1 small baked potato
Herbed Bean Salad*
Lemon Snow*
¼ pint (125 ml) skimmed milk
Coffee or tea

*These recipes are provided for you in the recipe section. See Index for page number.

Day 2

BREAKFAST—*236 calories*
1 medium fresh peach
Small portion of porridge
¼ pint (125 ml) skimmed milk
1 teaspoon sugar
Coffee or tea

LUNCH—*329 calories*
Cauliflower Caper Salad*
2 melba toast rounds
Marinated Fruit*
¼ pint (125 ml) skimmed milk
Coffee or tea

DINNER—*447 calories*
Fruited Chicken Breasts*
Average portion of spinach
Dill Tomato Slices*
1 crispbread
Rhubarb and Strawberry Bowl*
8 fluid oz (200 ml) skimmed milk
Coffee or tea

½ teaspoon butter or margarine
 allowed for the day

Day 3

BREAKFAST—*220 calories*
Average portion of melon
½ breakfast cup puffed wheat
4 tablespoons skimmed milk
1 teaspoon sugar
1 poached egg
Coffee or tea

LUNCH—*278 calories*
Crab Grill Deluxe*
Baked Crimson Pear*
¼ pint (125 ml) skimmed milk
Coffee or tea

DINNER—*496 calories*
Green Pepper Steak*
4 tablespoons cooked rice
Average helping of lettuce
1 tablespoon low-calorie dressing
Average portion of canned pineapple
8 fluid oz (200 ml) skimmed milk
Coffee or tea

½ teaspoon butter or margarine
 allowed for the day

Day 6

BREAKFAST—*202 calories*
¼ pint (125 ml) tomato juice
½ breakfast cup cornflakes
3 tablespoons skimmed milk
1 teaspoon sugar
1 crispbread
Coffee or tea

LUNCH—*270 calories*
French Onion Soup*
Dieter's Tuna Salad*
2 crispbreads
Average portion of melon
¼ pint (125 ml) skimmed milk
Coffee or tea

DINNER—*522 calories*
Italian Veal Cutlet*
Average portion of canned asparagus
Pineapple Mould Salad*
Raspberry-yogurt Fluff*
8 fluid oz (200 ml) skimmed milk
Coffee or tea

1 teaspoon butter or margarine
 allowed for the day

Day 7

BREAKFAST—*230 calories*
¼ pint (125 ml) tomato juice
Mushroom Omelette*
1 thin slice of brown bread
Coffee or tea

LUNCH—*270 calories*
Chicken-lettuce Salad*
Blackcurrant Ice*
8 fluid oz (200 ml) skimmed milk
Coffee or tea

DINNER—*507 calories*
Small cup of consommé
1 cream cracker
Oven-style Swiss Steak*
Broccoli Salad Bowl*
Strawberry-melon Parfait*
8 fluid oz (200 ml) skimmed milk
Coffee or tea

½ teaspoon butter or margarine
 allowed for the day

1200 Calorie Menus

Day 1

BREAKFAST—230 calories
½ grapefruit
½ breakfast cup puffed wheat
¼ pint (125 ml) skimmed milk
1 teaspoon sugar
1 poached egg
Coffee or tea

LUNCH—379 calories
Tuna-fruit Salad*
1 crispbread
Average portion of melon
8 fluid oz (200 ml) skimmed milk
Coffee or tea

DINNER—578 calories
Stuffed Steak Rolls*
Baked Stuffed Potato*
Average portion of lettuce
1 small tomato
1 tablespoon low-calorie dressing
Apple-ginger Bake*
8 fluid oz (200 ml) skimmed milk
Coffee or tea

Day 4

BREAKFAST—219 calories
1 small banana
½ breakfast cup bran-type cereal
¼ pint (125 ml) skimmed milk
1 teaspoon sugar
Coffee or tea

LUNCH—381 calories
Open Beefburger*
Blackcurrant Ice*
8 fluid oz (200 ml) skimmed milk
Coffee or tea

DINNER—612 calories
Ham in Peach Sauce*
½ medium baked potato
½ cup green beans
Orange Perfection Salad*
1 slice of wholemeal bread
Rhubarb and Strawberry Bowl*
¼ pint (125 ml) skimmed milk
Coffee or tea

1 teaspoon butter or margarine
  allowed for the day

Day 5

BREAKFAST—225 calories
¼ pint (125 ml) tomato juice
Small portion of porridge
3 tablespoons skimmed milk
1 slice of wholemeal toast
2 teaspoons sugar   Coffee or tea

LUNCH—396 calories
Hot Cheese-egg Sandwich*
1 small carrot and 1 celery stalk
Average portion of lettuce
1 tablespoon low-calorie dressing
8 fluid oz (200 ml) skimmed milk
2 fresh apricots   Coffee or tea

DINNER—579 calories
Fish with Italian Sauce*
4 tablespoons creamed potatoes
Average portion of green beans
Artichoke-fruit Salad*
Raspberry-apple Dessert*
8 fluid oz (200 ml) skimmed milk
1 slice of rye bread   Coffee or tea

2 teaspoons butter or margarine
  allowed for the day

*These recipes are provided for you in the recipe section. See Index for page number.

Day 2

BREAKFAST—*237 calories*

$\frac{1}{4}$ pint (125 ml) fresh orange juice
1 scrambled egg
1 slice of wholemeal toast
1 teaspoon diabetic jam
Coffee or tea

LUNCH—*381 calories*

Ham-asparagus Grill*
Average portion of lettuce
1 tablespoon low-calorie dressing
3 oz (75 gm) green grapes
8 fluid oz (200 ml) skimmed milk
Coffee or tea

DINNER—*575 calories*

London Grill*
Apple-flavoured Beetroot*
Oriental Spinach*
1 slice of rye bread
Mocha Chiffon*
8 fluid oz (200 ml) skimmed milk
Coffee or tea

2 teaspoons butter or margarine
    allowed for the day

Day 3

BREAKFAST—*222 calories*

$\frac{1}{2}$ pint (250 ml) tomato juice
1 boiled egg
1 slice of wholemeal toast
Coffee or tea

LUNCH—*428 calories*

Open Chicken Sandwich*
3 oz (75 gm) cottage cheese
1 medium grated carrot
1 medium fresh peach
8 fluid oz (200 ml) skimmed milk
Coffee or tea

DINNER—*569 calories*

Salmon Dolmas*
Average portion of peas
1 small tomato
1 slice of bread
Pineapple Dessert*
8 fluid oz (200 ml) skimmed milk
Coffee or tea

$1\frac{1}{2}$ teaspoons butter or margarine
    allowed for the day

Day 6

BREAKFAST—*224 calories*

Average portion of melon
1 boiled egg
1 slice of white toast
Coffee or tea

LUNCH—*362 calories*

Ham and Salad Roll*
2 medium fresh plums
8 fluid oz (200 gm) skimmed milk
Coffee or tea

DINNER—*615 calories*

Chicken in Tomato Sauce*
1 medium boiled potato
Sesame Broccoli*
Average portion of coleslaw
Marinated Fruit*
8 fluid oz (200 gm) skimmed milk
Coffee or tea

$2\frac{1}{2}$ teaspoons butter or margarine
    allowed for the day

Day 7

BREAKFAST—*217 calories*

$\frac{1}{4}$ pint (125 ml) grapefruit juice
$\frac{1}{2}$ breakfast cup cornflakes
3 tablespoons skimmed milk
1 slice of wholemeal toast
1 teaspoon sugar   Coffee or tea

LUNCH—*391 calories*

Crab-artichoke Toss*
3 oz (75 gm) fresh strawberries
Small slice of plain cake
$\frac{1}{2}$ pint (250 ml) skimmed milk
1 crispbread   Coffee or tea

DINNER—*596 calories*

$\frac{1}{4}$ pint (125 ml) grapefruit juice
Marinated Pot Roast*
Portion of turnips and carrots
Blender Cucumber Salad*
Peachy Orange Ice*
$\frac{1}{2}$ pint (250 ml) skimmed milk
Coffee or tea

$\frac{1}{2}$ teaspoon butter or margarine
    allowed for the day

1500 Calorie Menus

Day 1

BREAKFAST—334 calories

1 small orange
Average portion of porridge
8 fluid oz (200 ml) skimmed milk
2 teaspoons sugar   Coffee or tea

LUNCH—514 calories

Salmon-stuffed Tomato*
10 potato chips
1 medium grated carrot
$\frac{1}{4}$ pint (125 ml) skimmed milk
Snow Pudding*   Coffee or tea

DINNER—642 calories

$3\frac{1}{2}$ oz (87 gm) roast beef
Baked Stuffed Potato*
1 diced beetroot   Sauerkraut Salad*
1 slice of French bread
$\frac{1}{4}$ pint (125 ml) cold milk (to
    pour over strawberries)
3 oz (75 gm) fresh strawberries
$\frac{1}{4}$ pint (125 ml) skimmed milk
Coffee or tea

$1\frac{1}{2}$ teaspoons butter or margarine
    allowed for the day

Day 4

BREAKFAST—409 calories

Average portion of melon
1 teacup cornflakes   1 boiled egg
$1\frac{1}{2}$ teaspoons sugar
8 fluid oz (200 ml) skimmed milk
Coffee or tea

LUNCH—460 calories

Small portion of tomato soup
1 cheese sandwich
Average portion of lettuce
1 teaspoon low-calorie dressing
Apple-ginger Bake*   Coffee or tea

DINNER—638 calories

Orange-halibut Fillet*
4 tablespoons mashed potatoes
Creamy Brussels Sprouts*
Pineapple Mould*
1 small slice of bread
8 fluid oz (200 ml) skimmed milk
Baked Crimson Pear*   Coffee or tea

$1\frac{1}{2}$ teaspoons butter or margarine
    allowed for the day

Day 5

BREAKFAST—316 calories

$\frac{1}{4}$ pint (125 ml) tomato juice
1 poached egg   1 slice of toast
8 fluid oz (200 gm) skimmed milk
Coffee or tea

LUNCH—467 calories

Peach and Chicken Cup*
1 medium grated carrot
1 crispbread
Rice Pudding Royale*
$\frac{1}{4}$ pint (125 ml) skimmed milk
Coffee or tea

DINNER—709 calories

Pineapple-pork Chop*
4 tablespoons whole kernel corn
Apple-flavoured Beetroot*
$\frac{1}{2}$ medium fresh pear on a lettuce leaf
1 scone
Raspberry Bavarian Mould*
$\frac{1}{4}$ pint (125 ml) skimmed milk
Coffee or tea

$2\frac{1}{2}$ teaspoons butter or margarine
    allowed for the day

*These recipes are provided for you in the recipe section. See Index for page number.

Day 2

BREAKFAST—*315 calories*
½ pint (250 ml) tomato juice
1 scrambled egg
1 slice of white toast
8 fluid oz (200 gm) skimmed milk
Coffee or tea

LUNCH—*512 calories*
Macaroni-cheese Puff*
Carrot and Orange Salad*
1 medium fresh pear
8 fluid oz (200 ml) skimmed milk
Coffee or tea

DINNER—*678 calories*
3½ oz (87 gm) roast loin of pork
1 medium boiled potato
Average portion of green beans
Sunshine Apple Mould*
1 small roll
Grapefruit and Raspberry Compôte*
Coffee or tea

1 tablespoon butter or margarine
   allowed for the day

Day 3

BREAKFAST—*325 calories*
¼ pint (125 ml) orange juice
1 slice of toast
1 dessertspoon golden syrup
Coffee or tea

LUNCH—*507 calories*
Average portion of cream of
   celery soup
Devilled Hamburger*
Lemon-blackcurrant Fluff*
½ pint (250 ml) skimmed milk
Coffee or tea

DINNER—*679 calories*
Barbecued Rump Steak*
Onion and Potato Bake*
Basil Carrots*
Average portion of lettuce
1 tablespoon low-calorie dressing
Mocha Chiffon*
8 fluid oz (200 ml) skimmed milk
Coffee or tea

1½ teaspoons butter or margarine
   allowed for the day

Day 6

BREAKFAST—*334 calories*
Small portion of melon
2 thin slices of white bread
1 slice of grilled bacon
8 fluid oz (200 ml) skimmed milk
Coffee or tea

LUNCH—*541 calories*
Average portion of minced beef
Average portion of lettuce
1 small tomato
1 tablespoon low-calorie dressing
Baked Orange Cup*
8 fluid oz (200 ml) skimmed milk
1 sweet biscuit   Coffee or tea

DINNER—*641 calories*
Devilled Steak*
4 tablespoons creamed potatoes
Average portion of broccoli
Blender Cucumber Salad*
Lemon Snow*   2 wafer biscuits
1 slice of French bread   Coffee or tea

2 teaspoons butter or margarine
   allowed for the day

Day 7

BREAKFAST—*347 calories*
¼ pint (125 ml) grapefruit juice
1 boiled egg
2 rashers of grilled bacon
1 digestive biscuit   Coffee or tea

LUNCH—*558 calories*
Chicken-artichoke Bowl*
3 Italian bread sticks
Raspberry-yogurt Fluff*
8 fluid oz (200 ml) skimmed milk
Coffee or tea

DINNER—*596 calories*
Mushroom Cocktail*
Grilled Fillet Steak*
1 medium baked potato
Cauliflower Italiano*
Average portion of lettuce
1 tablespoon low-calorie dressing
Meringue-topped Peach*
8 fluid oz (200 ml) skimmed milk
Coffee or tea

½ teaspoon butter or margarine
   allowed for the day

1800 Calorie Menus

Day 1

BREAKFAST—*392 calories*

¼ pint (125 ml) grape juice
Average portion of porridge
1 teaspoon sugar
8 fluid oz (200 ml) skimmed milk
1 slice of white toast   Coffee or tea

LUNCH—*620 calories*

Chicken-artichoke Bowl*
14 potato chips
Rice Pudding Royale*
8 fluid oz (200 ml) skimmed milk
Coffee or tea

DINNER—*792 calories*

Curried Chicken*
4 tablespoons mashed potatoes
Peas with Mushrooms*
Sunshine Apple Mould*
Average portion of melon
3 tablespoons vanilla ice cream
1 dinner roll   Coffee or tea
2½ teaspoons butter or margarine
   allowed for the day

Day 4

BREAKFAST—*386 calories*

½ grapefruit
1 scrambled egg
1 slice of grilled bacon
8 fluid oz (200 ml) skimmed milk
1 slice of toast   Coffee or tea

LUNCH—*549 calories*

Cheese Soufflé*
Baked Devilled Tomato*
Yogurt-fruit Medley*
2 wafer biscuits
8 fluid oz (200 ml) skimmed milk
Coffee or tea

DINNER—*858 calories*

Onion-smothered Steak*
Vegetable Fiesta*
Broccoli Salad Bowl*
3 oz (75 gm) frozen raspberries
Small slice of plain cake
8 fluid oz (200 ml) skimmed milk
1 roll   Coffee or tea
1 tablespoon butter or margarine
   allowed for the day

Day 5

BREAKFAST—*416 calories*

½ pint (250 ml) tomato juice
1 slice of grilled gammon
1 boiled egg   1 slice of white toast
8 fluid oz (200 ml) skimmed milk
Coffee or tea

LUNCH—*547 calories*

Tangy Seafood Toss*
3 Italian bread sticks
Peachy Orange Ice*
8 fluid oz (200 ml) skimmed milk
Coffee or tea

DINNER—*836 calories*

Pineapple-pork Chops*
Average portion of marrow
Cheesy Onion Slices*
Average portion of lettuce
1 tablespoon low-calorie dressing
Small wedge of iced cake
8 fluid oz (200 ml) skimmed milk
1 dinner roll   Coffee or tea
4 teaspoons butter or margarine
   allowed for the day

*These recipes are provided for you in the recipe section. See Index for page number.

Day 2

BREAKFAST—*418 calories*

¼ pint (125 ml) orange juice
1 poached egg
¼ pint (125 ml) skimmed milk
1 roll   Coffee or tea

LUNCH—*514 calories*

Shrimp Stack-up*
1 medium grated carrot
4 tablespoons vanilla ice cream
2 tablespoons chocolate sauce
8 fluid oz (200 ml) skimmed milk
Coffee or tea

DINNER—*861 calories*

Basic Meat Loaf*
4 tablespoons creamed potatoes
Herbed Tomato Half*
Artichoke-fruit Salad*
Strawberry-melon Parfait*
8 fluid oz (200 ml) skimmed milk
1 roll   Coffee or tea

1 tablespoon butter or margarine
   allowed for the day

Day 3

BREAKFAST—*404 calories*

Average portion of melon
1 small kipper
2 teaspoons diabetic jam or marmalade
2 slices of white toast   Coffee or tea

LUNCH—*636 calories*

Turkey Hawaiian*
Dill Tomato Slices*
Lemon Snow*
8 fluid oz (200 ml) skimmed milk
1 wholemeal roll   Coffee or tea

DINNER—*773 calories*

Orange-glazed Lamb*
Baked Stuffed Potato*
Asparagus with Cheese*
Average portion of lettuce
1 tablespoon low-calorie dressing
1 slice of rye bread
Spicy Peach Compôte*
8 fluid oz (200 ml) skimmed milk
Coffee or tea

2 teaspoons butter or margarine
   allowed for the day

Day 6

BREAKFAST—*387 calories*

1 medium orange
Average portion of porridge
1 slice of wholemeal toast
8 fluid oz (200 ml) skimmed milk
1 teaspoon sugar   Coffee or tea

LUNCH—*571 calories*

Frankfurter-sauerkraut Bake*
Sunshine Aspic*
1 slice of rye bread
Glorified Rice*
8 fluid oz (200 ml) skimmed milk
Coffee or tea

DINNER—*847 calories*

Orange-halibut Fillet*
1 small baked potato
Green Beans with Onions*
Raspberry-cheese Mould*
Apple-ginger Bake*
8 fluid oz (200 ml) skimmed milk
1 scone   Coffee or tea

3½ teaspoons butter or margarine
   allowed for the day

Day 7

BREAKFAST—*465 calories*

¼ pint (125 ml) apple juice
1 scrambled egg   1 pork sausage
8 fluid oz (200 ml) skimmed milk
1 slice of toast   Coffee or tea

LUNCH—*563 calories*

Devilled Hamburger*
Asparagus Vinaigrette*
1 medium grated carrot
Baked Orange Cup*
8 fluid oz (200 ml) skimmed milk
Coffee or tea

DINNER—*772 calories*

French Onion Soup*
Marinated Beef Kebabs*
1 medium baked potato
Average portion of lettuce
1 tablespoon low-calorie dressing
1 slice of bread
8 fluid oz (200 ml) skimmed milk
Snow Pudding*   Coffee or tea

4 teaspoons butter or margarine
   allowed for the day

Low-calorie Entertaining

Do you have difficulty keeping the calories low when you entertain? Look through this section for party menus designed to flatter but not fatten. Whether it's a brunch, lunch, family dinner or buffet, diet-conscious guests are sure to voice their approval—and non-dieters will never suspect you're keeping a tally on calories. Serve the food buffet-style and let guests help themselves—a very important consideration for calorie-watchers.

Entertain guests at an evening buffet featuring Prawn Elegante, Fluffy Rice, Spinach and Artichoke Salad, French bread and dessert.

Entertaining at Lunch
Winter

```
+++++++++++++++++++++++++++++++++++++++
MENU

410 calories

Confetti Consommé
Hot Crunch Sticks
Beef Roll-ups
Mandarin and Pear Salad
Savoury Cottage Cheese
Coffee
+++++++++++++++++++++++++++++++++++++++
```

Confetti Consommé

22 calories per serving
A quick and tasty soup

- 2 cans condensed consommé
- ¾ pint (375 ml) water
- 1 large carrot, grated
- ½ small green pepper, chopped
- 1 small onion, finely chopped

In a medium saucepan combine consommé, water and vegetables. Bring to boil and serve hot. Serves 10.

Hot Crunch Sticks

70 calories per serving

An original accompaniment to any soup

- 1 breakfast cup cornflakes, crushed slightly
- 1 tablespoon poppy seeds
- 1 teaspoon salt
- Basic scone dough (made with 8 oz or 200 gm flour)

Mix cornflakes, poppy seeds and salt well together and put on to a sheet of greaseproof paper. Divide scone dough into 20 equal-sized pieces and roll between hands into 4 inch long sticks. Roll in cornflake mixture. Place sticks on a well greased baking tray and bake in a hot oven, Gas No 8 or 450°F (232°C), till lightly browned, about 8 to 10 minutes. Serve sticks warm. Makes 20.

Beef Roll-ups

121 calories per serving

- 10 slices cold roast beef
- 2 pickled cucumbers

Roll up slices of beef. Slice cucumbers into ½ inch pieces. Spear into 10 cocktail sticks and insert one into each beef roll. Makes 10.

Mandarin and Pear Salad

143 calories per serving

- ½ pint (250 ml) natural yogurt
- 2 tablespoons sugar
- 2 tablespoons blue cheese, crumbled
- 5 fresh medium pears, unpeeled, cored and halved
- Lettuce leaves
- 2 cans mandarin oranges, chilled and drained

In a small mixer bowl combine yogurt, sugar and 1 tablespoon of the blue cheese. Beat mixture with rotary beater or electric mixer till smooth. Sprinkle dressing with remaining crumbled blue cheese. Arrange pear halves on lettuce, and fill centres with mandarin sections. Accompany with blue cheese dressing. Serves 10.

Savoury Cottage Cheese

54 calories per serving

- 12 oz (300 gm) cottage cheese
- 12 stuffed olives
- 1 tablespoon drained capers
- 2 tablespoons very finely chopped parsley
- 3 level teaspoons paprika
- Salt and pepper to taste
- 2 inch lengths celery
- Cucumber slices

Rub cottage cheese through a sieve into a bowl. Beat in remaining ingredients. Serve with celery or cucumber slices. Serves 10.

```
+++++++++++++++++++++++++++++++++++
MENU

450 calories

Chilled Tomato Soup
Dressed Egg Salads
Crunchy Celery Toss
Peach Melba
Savoury Cheese Fingers
Coffee
+++++++++++++++++++++++++++++++++++
```

Chilled Tomato Soup

100 calories per serving

A special variation on tomato soup

- 2 cans condensed tomato soup
- 2 soup cans hot water
- 1 tablespoon Worcestershire sauce
- ¼ pint (125 ml) double cream
- 5 tablespoons dry sherry
- Chopped parsley or chives

Put soup into a large bowl and gradually beat in 2 cans of hot water. Leave until cold, then beat in remaining ingredients. Cover and chill for several hours. Before serving, stir well and transfer to soup cups. Serves 10.

Dressed Egg Salads

120 calories per serving

The dressing is an excellent slimming substitute for mayonnaise

- 10 large lettuce leaves
- 10 hard-boiled eggs
- ¾ pint (375 ml) natural yogurt
- ½ medium unpeeled cucumber, cut into tiny dice
- 4 tablespoons finely chopped parsley
- Liquid artificial sweetener to taste
- Salt and pepper to taste
- 5 small tomatoes, skinned and halved

Arrange lettuce on individual plates. Halve eggs and put two on to each plate, cut sides down. Beat yogurt with cucumber, parsley, sweetener, and salt and pepper to taste. Spoon equal amounts over egg halves and top each with a tomato half. Serves 10.

Crunchy Celery Toss

77 calories per serving

- 1 large head of celery
- 4 oz (100 gm) shelled walnuts
- 2 medium eating apples
- Lemon juice
- ¼ pint (125 ml) low-calorie dressing (page 8)

Wash celery stalks well, cut into thin diagonal slices and put into a large salad bowl. Chop nuts and add to bowl. Peel, core and slice apples, and brush each slice with lemon juice to prevent browning. Add to the bowl with dressing, and toss. Serves 10.

Peach Melba

80 calories per serving

Use frozen or canned raspberries out of season

- 5 large fresh peaches
- Lemon juice
- 8 oz (200 gm) fresh raspberries
- 10 scoops or tablespoons vanilla ice cream

Peel and halve peaches, and brush flesh with lemon juice to prevent browning. Sieve raspberries or blend until smooth in an electric blender. Put scoops or tablespoons of ice cream in sundae glasses. Add a peach half to each, and coat with raspberries. Serve straight away. Serves 10.

Savoury Cheese Fingers

73 calories per serving

- 6 oz (150 gm) Edam cheese, grated
- 1 egg yolk
- 1 teaspoon prepared mustard
- 3 slices of brown bread (each 1 oz or 25 gm)
- Cayenne pepper

Combine cheese with egg yolk and mustard. Toast bread on one side only and spread untoasted sides with cheese mixture. Sprinkle lightly with cayenne and brown under a hot grill. Cut into fingers and serve warm. Serves 10.

Weekend Brunch

MENU

463 calories

Double Juice Starter
Shirred Eggs Deluxe
Savoury Toast Puffed Triangles
Marmalade-toast Fingers
Melon Balls Melba
Coffee

Double Juice Starter

54 calories per serving

½ pint (250 ml) grapefruit juice
¾ pint (375 ml) tomato juice
Mint sprigs (optional)

Combine both juices and pour into six glasses containing a little crushed ice. Float mint sprigs on top if liked. Serves 6.

Marmalade-toast Fingers

20 calories per serving

6 slices of white bread, lightly toasted
3 tablespoons diabetic marmalade
1 teaspoon cinnamon

Trim crusts from toast. Combine marmalade and cinnamon, and spread on toast. Cut each slice into four strips. Grill 4 inches from heat till marmalade bubbles, about 1 minute. Serve piping hot. Makes 24 fingers.

Melon Balls Melba

63 calories per serving

¼ pint (125 ml) apple juice
1 teaspoon cornflour
Red food colouring
6 oz (150 gm) fresh raspberries
1 tablespoon sugar

1 medium melon, cut into balls
Mint sprigs

Gradually blend apple juice with cornflour. Cook, stirring, over medium heat till mixture is thick and bubbly. Remove from heat and colour deep pink with food colouring. Cool. Sprinkle fresh raspberries with sugar and spoon into sundae glasses with melon balls. Spoon on cooled apple sauce and garnish with mint sprigs. Serves 6.

Savoury Toast Puffed Triangles

74 calories per serving

4 oz (100 gm) Edam cheese, grated
1 egg, separated
1 teaspoon made mustard
1 teaspoon Worcestershire sauce
6 stuffed olives, finely chopped
6 slices of brown bread (each 1 oz or 25 gm)

Combine cheese with egg yolk and next three ingredients. Toast bread on one side only. Beat egg white stiffly, and fold into cheese mixture. Spread on untoasted sides of bread and brown under a hot grill. Cut into triangles. Makes 12.

Shirred Eggs Deluxe

252 calories per serving

1½ oz (37 gm) butter or margarine
12 eggs
Salt and pepper
4 oz (100 gm) fresh mushrooms, sliced
6 rashers bacon, crisp-cooked and crumbled
1 oz (25 gm) grated Parmesan cheese

Allowing 1 teaspoon each, butter six shallow individual casseroles. Break two eggs into each casserole, and add a dash of salt and pepper. Bake at Gas No 3 or 325°F (163°C) for 15 minutes. Top with mushrooms, crumbled bacon and cheese, then return to oven and bake for 5 minutes longer. Serves 6.

*Complete a weekend brunch with Melon Balls Melba—
honeysweet mouthfuls of melon and fresh raspberries
in apple juice sauce.*

Family Holiday Dinner

```
╔════════════════════════════╗
          MENU

        446 calories

   Holiday Cocktail Deluxe
 Roast Turkey    Rice Dressing
   Herbed Peas and Onions
   Orange and Cranberry Salad
        Pineapple Fluff
         Coffee or Tea
╚════════════════════════════╝
```

tender, about 20 minutes. Remove from heat, and stir in remaining ingredients and ¼ pint (125 ml) water. Turn into a 2 pint (1 litre) casserole. Bake, covered, at Gas No 4 or 350°F (177°C) till heated through, about 30 minutes. Serves 8.

Herbed Peas and Onions

32 calories per serving

- 1 large packet frozen peas
- 8 oz (200 gm) small onions, cooked
- 1 tablespoon lemon juice
- ½ teaspoon basil

Cook peas according to directions on the packet, but do not drain. Add onions and heat through. Drain thoroughly. Combine lemon juice and basil, and pour over peas and onions. Toss lightly to coat vegetables. Serves 8.

Holiday Cocktail Deluxe

67 calories per serving

- 4 grapefruit, sectioned
- 3 tablespoons pomegranate seeds
- 1 tablespoon grenadine syrup
- 1 bottle low-calorie bitter lemon, chilled

In a bowl combine grapefruit sections, pomegranate seeds and grenadine syrup. Chill for at least 30 minutes, stirring once or twice. To serve, spoon fruit and syrup into sundae dishes. Slowly pour bitter lemon over fruit mixture. Serves 8.

Rice Dressing

34 calories per serving

- 4 oz (100 gm) uncooked long-grain rice
- 2 medium celery stalks, chopped
- 1 small onion, chopped
- 3 chicken stock cubes
- ¼ teaspoon salt
- ½ pint (250 ml) + ¼ pint (125 ml) water
- 1 can (1 lb or ½ kilo) bean sprouts, drained and rinsed
- 4 oz (100 gm) mushrooms, sliced
- ½ teaspoon poultry seasoning
- ⅛ teaspoon sage
- Dash of pepper

In a saucepan combine rice, celery, onion, stock cubes, salt and ½ pint (250 ml) water. Bring to boil, then reduce heat. Simmer, covered, till rice is

Roast Turkey

176 calories per serving

- 6–8 lb (3–4 kilo) turkey
- Salt
- Salad oil

Rinse turkey and pat dry. Sprinkle inside with salt, and truss. Place, breast side up, on a rack in a shallow roasting pan. Lightly rub skin with salad oil. Top loosely with foil, and press down lightly at end of drumsticks and neck, leaving air space between bird and foil. Bake at Gas No 3 or 325°F (163°C) till done, about 3½ to 4 hours. During last 45 minutes of roasting, remove turkey from the oven and cut band of skin or string between legs and tail, then continue roasting, uncovered, till turkey is tender. (When done, the drumstick moves up and down and twists easily in its socket.) Remove bird from the oven, and allow to stand for 15 minutes before carving. Allow about 3½ oz (87 gm) light meat for each dieter. Serves 8.

Orange and Cranberry Salad

64 calories per serving

1 lb (½ kilo) fresh cranberries
¾ pint (375 ml) water
Artificial sweetener to taste
2 envelopes (about 3 teaspoons) gelatine
½ teaspoon grated orange peel
4 small oranges, peeled and chopped
2 medium celery stalks, chopped

Put cranberries into a pan with water. Bring to boil and cook for 7 minutes. Sweeten to taste, add gelatine and stir till dissolved. Chill till half set. Fold in orange peel, oranges and celery. Turn into a 2½ to 3 pint mould, and chill till firm. Serves 8.

Pineapple Fluff

73 calories per serving

1 large can crushed pineapple
1 envelope (about 3 teaspoons) gelatine
2 oz (50 gm) sugar
3 tablespoons cold water
¼ teaspoon salt
2 unbeaten egg whites
3–4 drops yellow food colouring

Drain pineapple, reserving juice. Add water to reserved pineapple juice to make ½ pint (250 ml). In a medium saucepan combine gelatine, sugar, water and salt, and add the reserved pineapple juice mixture. Stir over low heat till gelatine and sugar dissolve. Remove from heat and chill in the refrigerator till mixture is partially set. Turn into a large mixer bowl, adding egg whites and yellow food colouring. Beat at high speed with an electric mixer till light and fluffy, about 5 minutes. Fold in pineapple and chill again till partially set. Turn into a 2½ pint (1¼ litre) mould, and chill till firm. Unmould to serve. Serves 8.

Serve golden-brown Roast Turkey as the centrepiece of a family holiday dinner. Calorie watchers should go for the delicious light meat.

Evening Buffet

Hot Tomato Refresher

35 calories per serving

Ideal as a help-yourself appetizer

2½ pints (1¼ litres) tomato juice
2 tablespoons lemon juice
2 teaspoons Worcestershire sauce
½ teaspoon ground allspice
Thin lemon slices (optional)

In a large saucepan combine tomato juice, lemon juice, Worcestershire sauce and allspice; heat through. Just before serving, float lemon slices on top of the hot drink, if liked. Serves 12.

Spinach and Artichoke Salad

78 calories per serving

A quickly-made, sophisticated salad

2 cans artichoke hearts, drained
½ pint (250 ml) low-calorie dressing (page 8)
3 hard-boiled eggs
2 lb (1 kilo) fresh spinach, shredded
1 large lettuce, shredded

Halve artichoke hearts and marinate in dressing for 1 hour in the refrigerator. Drain hearts, reserving dressing. Dice two of the eggs and sprinkle with salt. In a large salad bowl place spinach, lettuce, drained artichoke hearts and diced eggs; toss lightly with reserved dressing. Slice remaining egg and arrange over salad. Serves 12.

Prawn Elegante

152 calories per serving

50 large Dublin Bay prawns, already shelled
1 lb (½ kilo) sliced green beans, cooked
3 chicken stock cubes
1 pint (½ litre) boiling water
8 spring onions, chopped
3 tablespoons Soy sauce
1 teaspoon salt
4 tablespoons cornflour
3 tablespoons cold water
4 medium tomatoes, cut into eighths

Wash and dry prawns. Drain beans. In a large saucepan or casserole dissolve stock cubes in boiling water. Add prawns, onions, Soy sauce and salt. Return to boil and cook, uncovered, for 3 minutes, stirring the prawn mixture occasionally. Blend together cornflour and cold water, and stir into prawn mixture. Cook, stirring, till mixture thickens and bubbles. Add tomato wedges and beans and cook for 3 minutes longer. Serves 12.

Fluffy Rice

93 calories per serving

1 lb (½ kilo) uncooked long-grain rice
1½ pints (¾ litre) boiling water
1 teaspoon salt
Parsley

Put rice, water and salt into a saucepan and cover tightly. Bring to rapid boil, then reduce heat. Continue cooking for 12 to 15 minutes or till rice grains are tender, and are separate and fluffy (all the water should be absorbed as well). Turn into a warm dish and garnish with parsley. Serves 12.

Choose your prettiest glass serving bowl for elegant Fruit Melange. Combine and chill this colourful array of fresh and canned fruit in advance.

Fruit Melange

87 calories per serving

1 can (1 lb or ½ kilo) pitted dark sweet
   cherries, drained and halved
12 oz (300 gm) fresh strawberries,
   sliced
1 medium melon, cut into balls
1 medium can pineapple chunks, drained
4 tablespoons diabetic marmalade
3 tablespoons hot water
1 teaspoon finely chopped candied ginger

1 medium-large banana, sliced
Lemon juice
Fresh mint

Chill fruits, and layer cherries, strawberries, melon
and pineapple in a large glass bowl. Combine
marmalade, hot water and candied ginger. Spoon
over fruit, then chill. Arrange banana on top of
fruit mixture. (To keep banana from darkening, dip
in lemon juice mixed with a little water.) Garnish
with mint. Serves 12.

Weekend Buffet Brunch

¾ pint (375 ml) water
3 lb (1½ kilo) topside or rump steak
36 large fresh mushrooms
6 medium tomatoes, cut into sixths

Combine first five ingredients and bring to boil. Reduce heat and simmer for 5 minutes, then cool. Trim fat from meat and cut into 1 inch cubes. Add meat and mushrooms to marinade, and toss to coat. Cover and marinate in the refrigerator for several hours or overnight. Drain, reserving marinade. Thread skewers alternately with meat, mushrooms and tomatoes. Grill 3 inches from heat for 5 to 6 minutes, then brush with reserved marinade. Turn and grill for 4 to 5 minutes longer. Brush with marinade. Serves 12.

Gala Starter

91 calories per serving

6 large ripe dessert pears
Lemon juice
12 large oranges
24 stuffed olives, sliced
6 large tomatoes, skinned and chopped
¼ pint (125 ml) low-calorie dressing
   (page 8)
12 large lettuce leaves
Watercress

Peel, halve and core pears. Chop flesh and sprinkle with lemon juice to prevent browning. Put into a large bowl. Peel oranges and divide into segments by cutting in between membranes. Add to bowl with olives, tomatoes and dressing, and toss. Arrange lettuce over base and sides of 12 glasses. Fill with equal amounts of orange mixture and top each with a watercress sprig. Serves 12.

Marinated Beef Kebabs

219 calories per serving

1½ packets dry onion soup mix
3 beef stock cubes
3 teaspoons prepared horseradish
1 teaspoon paprika

Cheesy Potato Balls

96 calories per serving

2 lb (1 kilo) potatoes
1 oz (25 gm) instant low-fat milk
   granules
1 oz (25 gm) Parmesan cheese
2 teaspoons prepared mustard
2 teaspoons curry powder
1 teaspoon garlic salt
Salt and pepper to taste
2 egg yolks

Boil potatoes until tender, then drain. Return to pan and stand over low heat. Beat in all remaining ingredients. Shape into small balls when cool enough to handle. Stand on a buttered baking tray and bake at Gas No 5 or 375°F (191°C) for 15 to 20 minutes. Spear a cocktail stick into each. Serves 12.

Cucumber and Fennel Salad

18 calories per serving

2 large cucumbers
8 oz (200 gm) fennel
4 tablespoons chopped parsley

1 small onion, finely chopped
2 boxes of mustard and cress
½ pint (250 ml) low-calorie dressing
(page 8)

Thinly slice unpeeled cucumber and put into a large bowl. Grate fennel and add with all remaining ingredients. Toss. Serves 12.

Tomato Asparagus Toppers

47 calories per serving

4 large tomatoes, skinned
24 canned asparagus spears
4 tablespoons mayonnaise
Paprika

Cut tomatoes into thirds horizontally. Stand on a platter and top each with two asparagus spears, halved. Add equal amounts of mayonnaise to each, then sprinkle lightly with paprika. Serves 12.

Blackcurrant Ice

44 calories per serving

3 oz (75 gm) sugar
3 teaspoons gelatine
1 pint (½ litre) water
12 oz (300 gm) fresh blackcurrants
4 tablespoons lemon juice

In a saucepan combine sugar and gelatine, then stir in half the water (¼ pint or 250 ml). Heat, stirring, over medium heat until sugar and gelatine dissolve. Remove from heat and add remaining water, blackcurrants and lemon juice. Freeze in two empty ice cube trays till firm. Break into chunks and beat with an electric mixer until smooth. Return to trays and freeze until firm. Leave to stand at room temperature for 5 to 10 minutes before serving. Serves 12.

Rice Pudding Royale

110 calories per serving

½ pint (250 ml) skimmed milk
1¼ pints (¾ litre) water
6 oz (150 gm) uncooked long grain rice

4 oz (100 gm) sugar
¼ teaspoon salt
1 teaspoon grated lemon peel
½ teaspoon grated orange peel
1½ teaspoons vanilla essence
½ teaspoon almond essence
8 oz (200 gm) cottage cheese

In the top of a double saucepan combine milk and water. Add rice, sugar and salt. Cook, covered, over boiling water for 1 hour, stirring often. Uncover and cook till thickened, about 30 to 40 minutes. Remove from heat, and stir in grated peels and flavourings. Chill thoroughly. Beat cottage cheese and stir into rice mixture. Spoon into dessert dishes and sprinkle with grated orange peel, if liked. Serves 12.

Vegetable and Cheese Savoury

37 calories per serving

6 large celery stalks, each cut into 12
pieces
48 radishes
4 oz Edam cheese, cut into small cubes
1 grapefruit

Spear celery, radishes and cubes of cheese on cocktail sticks. Spear into grapefruit and stand on a platter.

Grape Finale

28 calories per serving

Cut a large bunch of black grapes into 2 oz (50 gm) portions and allow 1 per person.

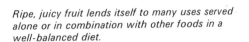

Ripe, juicy fruit lends itself to many uses served alone or in combination with other foods in a well-balanced diet.

Maintaining Your Weight

For further help in selecting low-calorie foods and keeping your weight down, use the handy cholesterol and calorie charts when planning your own shopping lists and menus.

The temptations for ignoring your diet are often greatest when eating out. For lunch, choose a low-calorie soup, open sandwiches, and plenty of fruit and vegetables. When eating out with friends, take larger helpings of low-calorie foods, and don't hesitate to leave calories on your plate—fat trimmed from meat, rich sauces, stuffings and dressings. In restaurants, avoid foods which are fried or served in a rich sauce, and omit bread, biscuits and heavy desserts.

Social drinking can be enjoyed even though you're counting calories. Learn to sip your drink slowly, avoiding the need for a refill. Remember—alcoholic calories must be added to your allowance and not used as a substitute for food. The chart on page 91 shows you how to plan your drinking.

CHOLESTEROL CHART

Cholesterol is present in all animal cells and is found in foods which are of animal origin. The cholesterol that appears in the food we eat is known as dietary cholesterol. The human body also manufactures cholesterol which is called body cholesterol. Although scientific research continues into the role of cholesterol in the body, the relationship between dietary cholesterol and body cholesterol is still not clearly defined.

Foods useful in low cholesterol diets include lean meat, lean fish, vegetables, fruit, bread, cereal, margarine, vegetable oil, cottage cheese, buttermilk, skimmed or non-fat milk and skimmed milk products. The chart overleaf lists the amount of dietary cholesterol, in milligrammes, which some of the more common foods contribute to the diet. The figures are based on a 100 gramme (4 oz) serving of each food.

FOOD	CHOLESTEROL Milligrammes per 100 grammes (4 oz)
Beef, raw	70
Brains, raw	2000
Butter	250
Caviare or fish roe	300
Cheese	
Cheddar	100
cottage, creamed	15
cream	120
other (25–30% fat)	85
Cheese spread	65
Chicken, flesh only, raw	60
Crab	125
Egg, whole	550
Egg, white	0
Egg yolk	
fresh	1500
frozen	1280
dried	2950
Fish	70
Heart, raw	150
Ice cream	45
Kidney, raw	375
Lamb, raw	70
Lard and other animal fats	95
Liver, raw	300
Lobster	200
Margarine	
all vegetable fat	0
two-thirds animal fat and one-third vegetable fat	65
Milk	
fluid, whole	11
dried, whole	85
fluid, skimmed	3
Mutton, raw	65
Oysters	200
Pork, raw	70
Prawns	125
Sweetbreads	250
Veal, raw	90

CALORIE CHART

	Calories
Anchovy, canned, 3 fillets	21
Apple	
baked, sweetened, 1 medium	188
fresh, 1 medium	70
juice, canned, $\frac{1}{2}$ pint (250 ml)	140
Apple charlotte, approximately 4 tablespoons	170
Apple sauce, canned	
sweetened, $\frac{1}{4}$ pint (125 ml)	145
unsweetened, $\frac{1}{4}$ pint (125 ml)	62
Apricots	
canned, $\frac{1}{2}$ pint (250 ml) in syrup	137
dried, cooked, unsweetened, $\frac{1}{2}$ pint (250 ml) in juice	150
fresh, 2–3 medium	51
nectar, $\frac{1}{2}$ pint (250 ml)	175
Arrowroot, 1 tablespoon	29
Asparagus	
canned, green, 6 medium spears	21
canned, white, 6 medium spears	21
cooked, $\frac{1}{4}$ pint (125 ml) cut spears	19
frozen, 6 spears	23
Aubergine (egg plant), uncooked, 1 lb ($\frac{1}{2}$ kilo)	64
Avocado, peeled, half	167
Bacon	
streaky rashers, 2 crisply grilled	96
very lean rashers, 3	195
Banana, 1 medium	85
Beans	
baked, with tomato sauce and pork, $\frac{1}{4}$ pint (125 ml)	200
broad, cooked, $\frac{1}{4}$ pint (125 ml)	162
green, runner or French, fresh, $\frac{1}{4}$ pint (125 ml)	20
green, as above, frozen, $3\frac{1}{2}$ oz (87 gm)	25
red kidney, canned or cooked, $\frac{1}{4}$ pint (125 ml)	145
yellow or wax, cooked, $\frac{1}{4}$ pint (125 ml)	14
Beef	
braising steak, lean and fat, 3 oz (75 gm)	245
braising steak, lean only, $2\frac{1}{2}$ oz (62 gm)	140
corned, canned, 3 oz (75 gm)	185
grilling steak, lean, 3 oz (75 gm)	220
minced beef, lean and fat, 4 oz (100 gm)	245
minced steak, lean, 4 oz (100 gm)	185
minced steak with onion and gravy, 4 oz (100 gm)	320
ox liver, fried, 2 oz (50 gm)	130
rib roast, lean and fat, 3 oz (75 gm)	375
rib roast, lean only, 3 oz (75 gm)	210
sirloin steak, grilled, 3 oz (75 gm)	330
stewed steak and gravy, 3 oz (75 gm)	78
tongue, cooked, 2 oz (50 gm)	210
Beetroot, cooked, diced, $\frac{1}{4}$ pint (125 ml)	27
Biscuits	
chocolate chip, 1 biscuit	52
chocolate fingers, 1 biscuit	28
cream crackers, 1 large biscuit	40
custard creams, 1 biscuit	59
digestive, 1 large biscuit	60
semi-sweet, such as Rich Tea, 1 biscuit	23
Blackberries, fresh, $\frac{1}{4}$ pint (125 ml)	50
Bread	
crispbread, 1 slice	30–40
French, 1 slice	58
rye, 1 slice	56
slimming, 1 slice	35–40
white, standard, 1 slice	62
wholemeal, 1 slice	56
Broccoli, 1 spear	29
Brussels sprouts, approximately 5	30
Butter, melted, 1 tablespoon	100
Cabbage	
cooked, $\frac{1}{4}$ pint (125 ml)	25
raw, shredded, $\frac{1}{2}$ pint (250 ml)	25
red, raw, shredded, $\frac{1}{2}$ pint (250 ml)	40
Cakes etc	
angel, thin slice	121
chocolate, two-layer, iced, 2 inch wedge	445
fruit, rich, 1 slice ($3 \times 3 \times \frac{1}{2}$ inch)	156
fruit, light, 1 slice ($3 \times 3 \times \frac{1}{2}$ inch)	152
gingerbread, 1 slice ($2 \times 2 \times 2$ inches)	175

Madeira, 1 thin slice	142
scone, 1, 2½ inches in diameter	140
sponge, no icing, 1 thin slice	149
Carrots	
cooked, diced, 3 oz (75 gm)	20
raw, 1 large or 2 small	42
Cauliflower, 4 oz (100 gm)	28
Celery, raw, 2 medium stalks	10
Cereals, raw	
barley, 1 oz (25 gm)	34
oatmeal porridge, 1 oz (25 gm)	13
rice, 1 oz (25 gm)	35
sago, 1 oz (25 gm)	101
semolina, 1 oz (25 gm)	100
tapioca, 1 oz (25 gm)	102
Cereals, breakfast	
all bran, 2 oz (50 gm)	176
cornflakes, 2 oz (50 gm)	208
shredded wheat, 2 oz (50 gm)	218
Cheese	
Camembert, 1 oz (25 gm)	88
Cheddar, 1 oz (25 gm)	120
Cheshire, 1 oz (25 gm)	110
cottage, 1 oz (25 gm)	33
cream, 1 oz (25 gm)	232
Danish blue, 1 oz (25 gm)	103
Edam, 1 oz (25 gm)	88
Gorgonzola, 1 oz (25 gm)	112
Gouda, 1 oz (25 gm)	96
Gruyère, 1 oz (25 gm)	132
Parmesan, 1 oz (25 gm)	118
processed, 1 oz (25 gm)	106
Stilton, 1 oz (25 gm)	135
Cherries	
canned, ¼ pint (125 ml)	111
stewed without sugar, 4 oz (100 gm)	40
unstoned, 4 oz (100 gm)	44
Chicken	
boiled, boneless, 1 oz (25 gm)	58
boiled, with bone, 4 oz (100 gm)	152
fricassee, 3½ oz (87 gm)	161
fried, dark meat, boneless, skinned, 3½ oz (87 gm)	220
fried, dark meat, boneless, with skin, 3½ oz (87 gm)	263
fried, light meat, boneless, skinned, 3½ oz (87 gm)	197
fried, light meat, boneless, with skin, 3½ oz (87 gm)	234
pie, individual, about 4½ inches in diameter	535
roast, boneless, 1 oz (25 gm)	54
roast, with bone, 4 oz (100 gm)	116
Chilli con carne with beans, canned, ¼ pint (125 ml)	208
Chilli sauce, 1 tablespoon	17
Chives, raw, chopped, 1 tablespoon	3
Chocolate	
bitter, 1 oz (25 gm)	142
milk, 1 oz (25 gm)	161
plain, 1 oz (25 gm)	160
Cocoa, 1 cup with milk	235
Cocoa powder, 1 tablespoon	21
Coconut, desiccated, 1 oz (25 gm)	178
Coffee, without milk or sugar	0
Corn	
fresh, 1 cob	85
whole kernel, drained, ¼ pint (125 ml)	106
Cornflour, 1 oz (25 gm)	100
Crab, 1 oz (25 gm), cooked, meat only	36
Cranberries	
fresh, 4 oz (100 gm)	16
sauce, canned, ½ pint (250 ml)	375
Cream	
Devon, 1 tablespoon	65
double, 1 tablespoon	65
single, 1 tablespoon	31
whipped, 1 tablespoon	25
Cress, watercress, 4 oz (100 gm)	16
Cucumber, about 6 slices	6
Currants	
black, fresh, 4 oz (100 gm)	32
dried, 1 oz (25 gm)	69
red, uncooked, 4 oz (100 gm)	24
Custard, made with powder, average portion	1( )
Damsons, fresh, 4 oz (100 gm)	45
Dates, stoned, 1 oz (25 gm)	95
Dill pickles, 2 oz (50 gm)	8
Doughnut, jam in centre	226
Dried milk	
skimmed, 1 oz (25 gm)	93
whole, 1 oz (25 gm)	150
Duckling, roast, 1 oz (25 gm)	89
Duck egg, 1 large	190
Eggs	
1 large, 2 oz (50 gm)	90
1 small	70
white, 1 oz (25 gm)	11
yolk, 1 oz (25 gm)	99
fried, 1 large	100
omelette, plain, 1 large egg	110
poached or boiled, 1 large	90
scrambled with milk, 1 large	110
Fats	
cooking fat, dripping, lard, margarine, suet, 1 oz (25 gm)	262
olive oil, 1 oz (25 gm)	264
Figs	
canned, with syrup, ¼ pint (125 ml)	137
dried, 1 large	60
raw, 3 small	90
Fish	
fish finger, 1	40
herring, 1 oz (25 gm)	67
kipper, 1 oz (25 gm)	62
salmon, canned, 1 oz (25 gm)	39
salmon, fresh, 1 oz (25 gm)	51
sardines, canned, 1 oz (25 gm)	84
white (haddock, cod, plaice etc), 1 oz (25 gm), boneless	20
as above, fried, 1 oz (25 gm)	58
Flour, wheat, 1 oz (25 gm)	100
Frankfurter, 1 large	155
Fruit cocktail, canned, with syrup, ¼ pint (125 ml)	100
Garlic, 1 clove	2
Gelatine, 1 oz (25 gm)	70
Ginger	
ale, ½ pint (250 ml)	100
crystallised, 1 oz (25 gm)	97
ground, 1 oz (25 gm)	74
Goose, roast, boneless, 1 oz (25 gm)	92
Gooseberries	
raw, cooking, 4 oz (100 gm)	20
ripe, dessert, 4 oz (100 gm)	40
Grapefruit	
canned, sections, with syrup, ¼ pint (125 ml)	100

fresh, medium, half	36
frozen, re-constituted, ½ pint (250 ml)	150
juice, canned, sweetened, ½ pint (250 ml)	163
juice, canned, unsweetened, ½ pint (250 ml)	125
Grapes	
black, 4 oz (100 gm)	56
juice, ½ pint (250 ml)	200
white, 4 oz (100 gm)	68
Gravy, 3 tablespoons	100
Greengages, with stones, 4 oz (100 gm)	52
Griddle cake or dropped scone, 1	60
Ham, cooked, lean, 1 oz (25 gm)	123
Honey, 1 tablespoon	60
Honeydew melon, 1 medium slice	50
Ice cream	
plain, 1 oz (25 gm)	56
sundae, average portion	410–440
Jam and marmalade, 1 oz (25 gm)	74
Ketchup, tomato, 1 tablespoon	18
Kidney	
lambs, 1 oz (25 gm)	28
ox, 1 oz (25 gm)	34
pigs, 1 oz (25 gm)	32
Lamb, lean, boneless, raw, 1 oz (25 gm)	97
Leek, cooked, 1 oz (25 gm)	7
Lemon juice, ¼ pint (125 ml)	8
Lemonade, small glass	36
Lentils, raw, 1 oz (25 gm)	84
Lettuce, round	24
Liver	
lambs, raw, 1 oz (25 gm)	39
ox and calves, raw, 1 oz (25 gm)	40
pigs, raw, 1 oz (25 gm)	43
Lobster, cooked, 1 oz (25 gm)	34
Luncheon meat, 1 oz (25 gm)	95
Macaroni, boiled, 1 oz (25 gm)	32
Mandarin oranges, canned, 1 oz (25 gm)	18
Marrow, boiled, 1 oz (25 gm)	2
Mayonnaise, 1 tablespoon	110
Maple syrup, 1 tablespoon	50
Marshmallows, 1 oz (25 gm)	90
Melba toast, 1 thin slice	15
Milk	
buttermilk, ½ pint (250 ml)	112
condensed, sweetened, whole milk 1 oz (25 gm)	100
evaporated milk, 1 oz (25 gm)	44
skimmed, ½ pint (250 ml)	100
whole, ½ pint (250 ml)	190
Mousse, frozen, small tub	120
Mushrooms, raw, 4 oz (100 gm)	8
Mussels, with shells, 8 oz (200 gm)	56
Nectarine, 1 medium	14
Noodles, egg, cooked, 1 oz (25 gm)	18
Nuts, mixed, unsalted, 1 oz (25 gm)	94
Oil	
corn, 1 tablespoon	130
olive, 1 tablespoon	130
Olives	
black, 10 large	80
green, with stones, 10 large	65
stuffed, 6 medium	70
Onions	
boiled, 1 oz (25 gm)	4
dried, 2 tablespoons	25
fried, 2 oz (50 gm)	202
raw, 1 oz (25 gm)	7
Orange	
fresh, 1 medium	40
frozen, re-constituted, ¼ pint (125 ml)	61
juice, canned, unsweetened, ¼ pint (125 ml)	75
juice, fresh, ¼ pint (125 ml)	72
Oysters, raw, 6 to 10 medium	80
Pancake, 1, 8 inches in diameter, no sugar	120
Parsley, fresh, 1 oz (25 gm)	6
Parsnip, cooked, diced, 3 oz (75 gm)	50
Partridge, roast, boneless, 1 oz (25 gm)	60
Pâté de foie, canned, 1 oz (25 gm)	132
Peaches	
canned, 2 halves and 2 tablespoons syrup	90
fresh, 1 medium	36
Peanut butter, 1 oz (25 gm)	180
Pears	
canned, 2 medium halves and 2 tablespoons syrup	90
fresh, 1 medium	34
Peas	
canned, 1 oz (25 gm)	24
dried, boiled, 1 oz (25 gm)	28
fresh green, boiled, 1 oz (25 gm)	14
split, boiled, 1 oz (25 gm)	33
Pepper, green, raw, 1 medium	10
Pickle	
sour, 4 oz (100 gm)	22
sweet, 4 oz (100 gm)	158
Pies	
apple, average helping	410
cherry, average helping	418
custard, average helping	327
lemon meringue, average helping	357
mince, average helping	434
Pimiento, canned, 1 medium	10
Pineapple	
canned, with syrup, 2 oz (50 gm)	44
crystallised, 1½ oz (37 gm)	120
fresh, 1 slice, 2 oz (50 gm)	26
juice, small glass	53
Pistachio nuts, 1 oz (25 gm)	168
Plums	
canned, 3 whole plums and 2 tablespoons syrup	92
fresh dessert, 1 large	18
stewed, without sugar, 8 oz (200 gm)	48
Popcorn	
plain, 2 oz (50 gm)	275
sugar coated, 2 oz (50 gm)	268
Popover (individual Yorkshire pudding)	112
Pomegranate, fresh, 1 medium	63
Pork	
sausages, fried, 2 oz (50 gm)	186
lean chop, grilled, 4 oz (100 gm)	152
roast leg, 1 oz (25 gm)	90
roast loin, meat and fat, 1 oz (25 gm)	129
Potato crisps, average packet, 1 oz (25 gm)	161
Potatoes	
baked in jacket, 1 medium	96
chips, 1 oz (25 gm)	68

creamed, 1 tablespoon	16
new, boiled, 1 oz (25 gm)	21
old, boiled, 1 oz (25 gm)	23
roast, 2 small pieces	140
Prawns, 3 oz (75 gm)	100
Prunes	
raw, 4 oz (100 gm)	152
stewed, without sugar, 4 oz (100 gm)	76
Pudding	
canned, sultana, fruit or sponge, 1 oz (25 gm)	88
instant, made up as directed, ¼ pint (125 ml)	175
Rabbit	
roast, meat only, 4 oz (100 gm)	202
stewed, with bones, 4 oz (100 gm)	104
Radishes, 4 small	5
Raisins, 1 oz (25 gm)	70
Raspberries	
canned with syrup, 2 oz (50 gm)	50
fresh, raw, 1 oz (25 gm)	7
frozen, sweetened, ¼ pint (125 ml)	150
Rhubarb, raw, 4 oz (100 gm)	8
Rolls	
1, crusty, 2 oz (50 gm)	160
1, hamburger bun, 2 oz (50 gm)	89
1, starch reduced, 2 oz (50 gm)	27
1, wholemeal, 2 oz (50 gm)	98
Sauerkraut, drained, 4 oz (100 gm)	30
Scallops	
fried, 4 oz (100 gm)	295
grilled, 4 oz (100 gm)	175
steamed, 4 oz (100 gm)	120
Scampi, fried, 4 oz (100 gm)	250
Skate, fried, 1 oz (25 gm)	69
Snails, with garlic butter, 3 medium	100
Soy sauce, 1 tablespoon	10
Spaghetti, raw, 1 oz (25 gm)	104
Spinach, boiled, 4 oz (100 gm)	28
Sprats	
fresh, fried with heads, 1 oz (25 gm)	111
smoked, 4 oz (100 gm)	324
Spring greens, boiled, 4 oz (100 gm)	12
Stock cubes, approximately 1	16
Strawberries	
canned, 4 oz (100 gm), with syrup	90
fresh, 4 oz (100 gm)	28
frozen, sweetened, ¼ pint (125 ml)	175
Sugar	
Demerara, 1 oz (25 gm)	111
white, 1 oz (25 gm)	112
Sweets, assorted	
boiled, 1 oz (25 gm)	100
caramels, 1 oz (25 gm)	115
chocolate creams, 1 oz (25 gm)	120
chocolate peanuts and raisins, 1 oz (25 gm)	143
chocolate truffles, 1 oz (25 gm)	120
fruit gums, 1 oz (25 gm)	50
nougat, 1 oz (25 gm)	122
Tangerine, fresh, 1 medium	21
Tomatoes	
canned, ¼ pint (125 ml)	31
fried, 2 oz (50 gm)	40
juice, canned, ½ pint (250 ml)	50
paste or concentrate, 1 oz (25 gm)	24
raw, fresh, 1 oz (25 gm)	4
Treacle, black, 1 tablespoon	36

Tripe, cooked, 4 oz (100 gm)	116
Trout	
smoked, 4 oz (100 gm)	134
steamed or poached, whole fish, 4 oz (100 gm)	100
Tuna, canned, drained, 1 oz (25 gm)	56
Turkey, roast, 1 oz (25 gm)	56
Turnips, cooked, 4 oz (100 gm)	12
Veal	
escalope, 3 oz (75 gm)	184
as above, coated with egg and breadcrumbs	220
kidneys, raw, 1 oz (25 gm)	40
roast, 1 oz (25 gm)	70
stewed, 1 oz (25 gm)	60
Vinegar, 1 tablespoon	2
Waffle, 1 medium	220
Walnuts, shelled, 1 oz (25 gm)	156
Water chestnuts, 4	20
Watermelon, 1 medium slice	115
Wheat germ, 1 tablespoon	15
Whitebait, fried, 1 oz (25 gm)	152
Yogurt	
fat-free, ¼ pint (125 ml)	71
flavoured, ¼ pint (125 ml)	120
natural, ¼ pint (125 ml)	75
real fruit, ¼ pint (125 ml)	160

ALCOHOLIC DRINKS CHART

This chart gives the average calorific value of unmixed alcoholic drinks. If drinks are mixed, the other ingredients must be added. However, low-calorie carbonated beverages (bitter lemon, ginger and tonic) are available, and the calorific value of these is negligible.

	Calories
Bacardi, 1 measure	63
Beer, Bitter, ½ pint (250 ml)	210
Beer, Pale Ale, ½ pint (250 ml)	155
Benedictine, liqueur glass	75
Brandy, liqueur glass	75
Champagne, small glass	90
Cherry brandy, liqueur glass	90
Cider, dry, ½ pint (250 ml)	100
Cider, sweet, ½ pint (250 ml)	120
Crème de menthe, liqueur glass	90
Dubonnet, average glass	165
Drambuie, liqueur glass	65
Gin, 1 measure	55
Guinness, ½ pint (250 ml)	210
Madeira, small glass	110
Port, small glass	165
Rum, dark, 1 measure	75
Sherry, dry, average glass	65
Sherry, medium, average glass	70
Sherry, sweet, average glass	75
Vermouth, dry, average glass	110
Vermouth, sweet, average glass	175
Vodka, 1 measure	63
Whiskey, Irish, 1 measure	63
Whisky, Scotch, 1 measure	58
Wine, dry red, small glass	70
Wine, dry white, small glass	65
Wine, rosé, small glass	70
Wine, sweet white, small glass	90

Index

BASIC METHODS OF COOKING

BAKING—cooking in dry heat in the oven.

BOILING—cooking food in a boiling liquid (212°F), eg. vegetables, pasta and boiled puddings.

BRAISING—meat is browned then cooked slowly on a bed of vegetables with very little liquid, in a covered container.

FRYING—Shallow frying is cooking in just enough fat to cover the base of the pan. It is a quick method of cooking.
Deep frying is cooking food by immersing in a deep pan filled two-thirds full of hot fat or oil.

GRILLING—always pre-heat the grill for this method of cooking and brush the grill rack with fat. Food which is to be completely cooked by grilling should be cooked at a high temperature for the initial browning period. Then reduce the heat and complete the cooking.

POACHING—cooking food gently in liquid at simmering temperature (185-200°F).

POT ROASTING—a combination of frying and steaming. The meat is browned and then cooked in a heavy covered casserole or saucepan with fat only. It is a slow method of roasting and may be carried out on top of the stove or in the oven at a low temperature.

PRESSURE COOKING—cooking food at a very high temperature under pressure. The food cooks quickly and tougher types of meat are made more tender. Types of pressure cookers vary and the makers instructions should be followed exactly.

ROASTING—cooking food at a high temperature in the oven. The container is open and little fat should be used.

SAUTÉ—To cook over a strong heat in a small amount of fat or oil, shaking the pan frequently to prevent sticking.

SIMMERING—cooking below boiling point—the liquid should bubble gently at the side of the pot.

STEAMING—using the steam from boiling water to cook food. The food may be cooked in a steamer over boiling water or the basin of food may be stood in the boiling water. Always cover the saucepan or steamer.

STEWING—cooking food at simmering point or below in a liquid. It is a long slow method of cooking and an excellent way of tenderising the tougher cuts of meat. Stewing is carried out in a covered container.

COOKING TERMS

BAIN MARIE—a roasting tin half filled with water in which a dish of food which must be baked slowly is placed before cooking in the oven, e.g. caramel custards.

BAKING BLIND—the method of baking flans, tarts and other pastry cases without a filling. Put the flan ring or pie dish on a baking sheet and line with pastry. Cut a circle of greaseproof paper slightly larger than the flan. Fill with dried beans, rice, or bread crusts to weigh the paper down. Bake the flan for 15 minutes. Remove the greaseproof paper and beans and bake a further 10 minutes to brown and crisp the pastry. Cool.

BASTING—spooning the cooking fat and liquid over food while roasting. This keeps the food moist, adds flavour and improves the appearance.

BEATING—method of introducing air to a mixture, a wooden spoon, wire whisk or electric beater may be used for this process.

BINDING—adding a liquid, egg or melted fat to a dry mixture to hold it together, e.g. beaten egg is added to mince for hamburgers.

BLANCHING—putting food in boiling water in order to either whiten, remove the skin, salt or strong flavour from food.

BLENDING—the process of mixing a thickening agent, such as flour or cornflour with a little cold water to a smooth paste. A little of the hot liquid to be thickened is then added to the paste and the whole returned to the saucepan. The mixture is stirred until it boils and thickens. Used to thicken the liquid of casseroles, stews and certain sauces.

BOUQUET GARNI—a bunch of fresh mixed herbs tied together with string and used for flavouring. Usually a bay leaf, sprig of parsley, sprig of thyme and perhaps a few celery leaves. Dried herbs may be used tied in a little muslin bag.

BROWNING—putting a cooked dish or meringue under the grill, or in the oven for a short time to give it an appetising golden colour.

CASSEROLE—baking dish usually ovenproof earthenware, pottery, porcelain or cast-iron with a tight fitting lid. Food cooked in a casserole is served straight from the dish.

CHINING—method of preparing neck or loin joints for easier carving. The bone at the wide end of the chops or cutlets is cut away from the meat so that it may be carved into portions of one rib each.

CHOPPING—dividing food into very small pieces on a chopping board using a very sharp knife.

COATING—covering food with a thin layer of flour, egg, breadcrumbs or batter before it is fried.

CONSISTENCY—term describing the texture (usually the thickness) of a mixture.

CREAMING—beating together fat and sugar to incorporate air, break down the sugar crystals and soften the fat.

CUTTING IN—Usually applies to adding fat to pastry. Fat is cut into flour with a knife.

FOLDING IN—to incorporate two mixtures using a light over and over motion. Usually applied to light mixtures such as whisked egg white or cream which have to be folded into other ingredients. It is important to carry out the process carefully so that the air is not knocked out of the light mixture. Flour is sifted over whisked egg mixtures for very light sponge cakes. The use of an electric mixer is not practical for this process. A sharp edged metal spoon is ideal for folding in.

GLAZE—a liquid brushed over the surface of a dish to give it a shiny finish.

GRATE—shaving food into shreds.

HULL—remove stalks from soft fruits—strawberries, raspberries etc.

KNEADING—working a dough using the fingertips for pastry-making and the knuckles for bread-making. The edges of the dough are drawn to the centre.

KNOCKING BACK—This applies to yeast mixtures which have had one rising. The dough is turned out, kneaded with the hands and reshaped.

MARINADE—a liquid made of oil and wine, vinegar or lemon juice and flavouring vegetables, herbs and spices. Food is steeped in the marinade to tenderise and add flavour.

PURÉE—fresh or cooked fruit or vegetables are broken down into a smooth pulp by sieving, pounding or blending in the liquidiser.

REDUCING—boiling a liquid, uncovered, in order to evaporate the water content and make the liquid more concentrated.

ROUX—a thickening agent for soups and sauces. Equal quantities of fat and flour are cooked together.

RUBBING IN—a method of incorporating fat into flour, e.g. in short-crust pastry making. Add the fat in small pieces to the flour. Using the fingertips, quickly and lightly rub the fat into the flour, lifting the hands as you do this.

SEASONED FLOUR—mix 1 teaspoon of salt, a good sprinkling of pepper and 2 tablespoons of flour. Use to coat food before cooking.

SIEVING—to rub food through a sieve using a wooden spoon, in order to discard skin, stalks or seeds.

SKIMMING—to remove the scum or fat from food whilst it is cooking. A piece of absorbent kitchen paper or a metal spoon are used.

STOCK—a well-flavoured liquid made by simmering meat and/or vegetables in water for a prolonged period, to extract the flavour. When time is short the commercial stock cubes may be substituted.

SWEATING—cooking foods, usually vegetables in a small amount of fat to soften and add flavour. The pan is always covered.

WATER BATH—see Bain marie.

WHIPPING OR WHISKING—adding air quickly to a mixture by beating with a hand whisk, rotary beater or electric beater.

ZEST—the thin coloured skin of citrus fruit which contains the oil and flavour.